STORIES OF

VETERANS

FROM MILITARY TO CIVILIAN LIFE

Compiled by *Dr. Trunnis Goggins II*

Published By: DNP Publishing

Library of Congress Cataloging-in-Publication Data has been applied for

ISBN: 979-8-3306-6468-9

PRINTED IN THE UNITED STATES OF AMERICA

TABLE OF CONTENTS

THE STORY OF VETERAN

TRUNNIS GOGGINS II

IT'S NOT JUST A JOB.
IT'S AN ADVENTURE.

Back in the 1980s, the United States Navy had a recruiting commercial, and at the end of that commercial, there was the slogan, "It's not just a job; it's an adventure." I must admit it was a very catchy slogan. Not only was it popular for recruiting, but the slogan became trendy for multiple uses back then. Though the United States Navy used it as a recruiting commercial, that slogan rings true for all of the other military branches. Being in the United States military is certainly not just a job. It is an adventure like no other, and if you take advantage of all the opportunities the military offers, you will never find professional satisfaction in quite the same way. Because of this and other issues, many people find the transition from military life to civilian life so difficult.

I am not a traditional Navy veteran. I did not join the Navy, like so many others, right after high school. I was much older. As a matter of fact, I went out and had jobs, tried college, and even got married before joining. Because of my familiarity with civilian life, my transition back into civilian life should have been way easier. However, that was the case. Transition from military back to civilian life was filled with uncertainty, dissatisfaction, and even depression. These feelings are not uncommon when it comes to service members returning to civilian life. We all know that several pitfalls service members encounter.

I joined the United States Navy as an adult. I spent the beginning of my Navy career as a reservist. I truly loved being a part of the military, even though it was on a part-time basis. Like so many military members, I was recalled to active duty after 9/11. At the time, I recall, I was a paralegal for the Indiana Atty. Gen.'s office, so when recalled the first time, I assisted in the preparation of wills and power of attorneys for recalled Sailors and Marines. I also assisted in making sure that the recalled reservist received adequate protection under the Soldiers and Sailors Act. I was recalled a second time in May 2003, and at that time I was recalled being a prior service recruiter.

Leaving the Indiana Atty. Gen.'s office was bittersweet. I loved my time at the office and developed lifelong friendships while serving there. However, I will have to say that my time working for the Navy Reserve Recruiting Command (Area Central), particularly Zone Five, was the greatest job I ever had. From top to bottom, that command was impeccable. I met lifelong friends there as well. One person in particular, NCC Buck Campfield, changed my life forever. I share my story about him in the book *The 4P's of You*. I served as a Navy recruiter under three different commands. The last part of my service was as a recruiter in charge.

Currently, I wear many hats. I am an author, I am a consultant, I am a public speaker, and I am a college professor in business. I teach organizational behavior courses, and I will say that using the concepts that I teach in college, organizational behavior in military institutions is much, much different than organizational behavior in civilian life. This can have a profound effect on service members leaving the military and transitioning into civilian life professionally.

As I previously said, working for NRRC (Area Central) was the greatest job ever had in my life. I will say that in addition to Chief Campfield, the other individuals I worked for in that office were just as influential as he was at the time. When I started recruiting, our office consisted of five recruiters. We were not just coworkers we were legitimately family. Even to this day, though we do not talk as often as we should, I know if any of us needed anything at all, we would be there. During my time in that office, we all got to know each other and became brothers and sisters.

When I we became family, I truly mean we became family. Not only did we work together, but we attended cookouts and family gatherings. We were there for each other's children, and we were there for each other. There are so many things that the recruiting office did personally and professionally. We grew to look out for each other in almost every way possible. This type of dynamic is not rare in the military community. As a matter of fact, it is almost commonplace. Military members share and have experienced challenges (not necessarily combat) that many civilians will never experience as a unit. These experiences with military members lead to a certain connection. Even now, if I see a veteran, whether I know them or not, I have a certain connection with that person.

When talking to veterans, I often hear them reminiscing and longing for that type of connection in their civilian professions. One thing that I've come to realize is that that working connection is almost exclusively a connection that is established in military and first responder professions. Though there are many strong connections in the civilian sector, those types of connections are virtually nonexistent. Service members, when getting out of the military, should be warned of this professional cultural difference by my fellow veterans and military counselors before leaving the military. This warning may assist new veterans in professionally adjusting to their newly found civilian careers.

When I was a recruiter in the central Indiana area, one thing I remembered was the recognition I received from civilians while I was walking in uniform. I was recruiting during Operation Enduring Freedom and the war on terror. I remember walking down the street and people thanking me for my service. I went home every single day after work, knowing that I was doing something for my community and for my nation. No, I did not feel like a hero, but I did feel like I could play my part to keep my generation and future generations of Americans free. I truly felt a high level of job satisfaction.

When I got out of the Navy, I briefly went back to the Indiana Atty. Gen.'s office and assumed my job as a paralegal. My ultimate goal was to get into higher education, and I did not have all my credentials to make that move immediately after leaving the Navy. As I previously mentioned, before joining the Navy, my job at the Indiana Atty. Gen.'s office gave me a great deal of satisfaction. I truly felt that I was doing something for the state of Indiana. However, when I returned to my old position, I did not feel any type of satisfaction at all. As a matter of fact, I didn't feel that I belonged in that position. I did not feel that I was doing anything to help make the state better. I truly felt that I was going through the motions. This feeling led to a professional depression.

It is important that service members realize that in the civilian world, you still have a mission. In the military, you wear a uniform; there are clearly defined objectives and orders in missions that you, as a service member, are assigned to achieve. Your mere title as a soldier, sailor, airman, and Marine gives you a clear perspective of who you are and what you are meant to do. That clarity, though it is there, is not as visible and well-defined in the civilian world. This lack of clarity can lead to a lack of direction. The lack of direction can lead to dissatisfaction. The dissatisfaction can lead to or even contribute to depression after leaving the military. Once again, these are issues that should be addressed when service members are preparing to separate from the United States military.

The other issue that leads to a level of professional depression is the fact that there is a misconception about true salary. Back when I was in the Navy, I remember my base pay was roughly $2800 a month. However, with all of the benefits, such as a basic allowance for housing, a basic allowance for food, and special duty pay, I was making close to $70,000 a year. Back in 2008, that was great money. In addition, some of those benefits were not taxed, so I was only getting taxed on less than 50% of my total salary. When leaving the military, that was not wholly considered. When I got out of the Navy and negotiated my first civilian salary in quite some time, I put my family and myself in a precarious financial situation.

It is imperative that service members understand that they are preparing to separate from the military and that they truly understand all the financial aspects to consider when beginning their transition back to civilian life. I do believe that financial misconceptions held by military members are one of the components leading to service members facing severe financial hardships that can sometimes lead to bankruptcy and homelessness.

The purpose of this book is to serve as a supplemental reference for service members leaving the United States military. This is one of the hardest transitions that a person will ever go through. There are so many things that must be considered when making this transition. Think about it: depending on your job in the United States military, it can take the government up to two years to get you fully trained to be an effective servicemember. However, the military often gives you a month or less to "train" to be an effective civilian once leaving the military. This lack of training can prove disastrous, at least in the initial stages of this transition.

This book is in no way an attempt to paint the military in a bad light. On the contrary, this book is designed to make sure that your imminent transition back into the civilian world is as smooth as possible. This book is a story of members from different branches in different eras. These brothers and sisters share their stories with you to let you know that you are not alone in this transition. For example, when you were wearing the uniform, you knew that there were those who had your back. I want you to know that the oath you swore at your initial enlistment or commission never expires. And that family, that brotherhood and sisterhood, does not disappear once our uniform becomes blue jeans and hoodies.

I have said before that the best experience I ever had in my life was being a member of the United States military. Just recently, my son Nicholas Goggins followed in his father's and uncle's footsteps and enlisted in the United States Navy.' I told him that this will truly be an experience you will never forget. I also warned him that this is an experience that he will truly never be able to replicate. Being a part of the United States military is a privilege that not many are awarded. It is also a responsibility to our fellow members that never goes away.

Just like your oath never expires, the resources provided in this book and the authors who wrote in this book will always be here to help you during this transition now and in the future. I hope you enjoy.

DR. TRUNNIS GOGGINS II

NAVY

PETTY OFFICER 2ND CLASS

Connect with Trunnis

trunnis@trunnisgoggins2.com

THE STORY OF VETERAN

BY DR. SONYA HOWELL BARROW

SOLDIER GIRL

*"And the LORD, he it is that doth go before thee;
he will be with thee, he will not fail thee, neither
forsake thee: fear not, neither be dismayed."*

KJV Deuteronomy 31:8

"My silence does not represent my defeat.
Instead, it ignites every element of my FIRE. *I am*
FEARLESS. INSPIRED. RESILIENT. EMPOWERED."

~ Dr. Sonya Howell Barrow

As I relaxed on the balcony of my hotel room located at the heart of Waikiki, I became enchanted with the warm breeze from the ocean, its aroma filled with salt and tropical flowers. The calming sounds of waves that splashed on the shore complimented the intermittent pop of the Friday night fireworks that illuminated the evening sky. I watched as vibrant colors erupted in the distance, their radiant images swirled across the beautiful turquoise waters and cast a glow that seamlessly blended with the hues of the evening sunset. Though I appreciated being surrounded by the natural beauty of palm trees that swayed lazily as their leaves gently whispered in the wind, my thoughts continuously wandered away.

Each firework that burst in the sky pulled me further into a flood of memories. Though my eyes were enchanted with the spectacular display of colors, a deeper reflection took hold of my thoughts. I was reminded that although I enjoy the display of fireworks, I can only enjoy the sound of fireworks from a safe distance away. Unfortunately for me, a United States Army Combat Veteran who served two tours in support of Operation Iraqi Freedom (OIF) and two tours in support of Operation Enduring Freedom (OEF), loud and explosive firework blasts significantly enhance my Post-Traumatic Stress Disorder (PTSD). Hmm, I thought to myself, "How did I survive the stressful life of a Soldier?" Then, I smiled as I was reminded of God's grace and mercy.

As the ocean waves rolled in, fireworks shimmered across the sky and faded; I realized my stunning views contrasted with the rigid structure of *"soldier girl."* Suddenly, my thoughts transcended me back to October 15, 1992, and the Army Recruiting Station located in Southgate Plaza on Gordon Highway in my hometown of Augusta, Georgia. This was the day that a 20-year-old frightened young mother joined the United States Army in order to escape from poverty. *"She Is Me!"*

The sounds of excitement and laughter floated up from Waikiki Beach and blended harmoniously with soft bursts of fireworks in the night sky. While fireworks exploded in the distance, my private thoughts exploded into painful memories. As I looked down and observed families gathered for nighttime festivities with their young children, I was reminded of the milestone moments and festivities that I missed throughout the years. Sadly, I've missed countless birthdays, holidays, first days of school, and other important events with my children during times when they needed me the most. Unfortunately, due to military obligations, I was oceans away. Each time the sky lit up, I felt a wave of nostalgia, pride from serving my country, and the bittersweet sadness of the time lost with the two most important people in my life, my children, who are my heartbeats.

Life is short, and *time* is precious. As I looked around tearfully, I was reminded of the lost *time* that I will never be able to get back. All I can do now is strive to make the most of every moment with my children, other family members, and friends. Moments of joy and reunion, though brief, felt bright as I observed the final boom of fireworks as they disappeared into the night. As the last firework transcended across the sky, followed by the grand finale of vibrant colors across the ocean, I felt a sense of calmness. This tranquil setting provided me with a moment of silence. So, I paused, took a deep breath, quickly prayed, then exhaled.

With a slight grimace, easily mistaken for a smile, I reflected on my 26+ years of Active-Duty service in the United States Army, much of it spent as a single parent. With every decision and sacrifice, I was determined to remain *fearless, inspired, resilient, and empowered*, always striving to do what was best for me and my children. As I reflected on my past, I realized that the challenges, sacrifices, and lost *time* had ultimately led me to a place where I could finally reflect, heal, and truly understand the deep cost of military service, for myself, my children, and my family. Ultimately, *"soldier girl"* remains in every reflection of me, like an echo carried on the ocean breeze.

Becoming Soldier Girl

After the fireworks faded into the night sky, I walked along the beach, the cool sand shifted beneath my feet as gentle waves lapped at the shore in tune with the live music that played in the background. The sky, still faintly illuminated by the remnants of the colorful display, mirrored the reflections that stirred within me. With each step, memories of my childhood flooded back.

From the very beginning, my life had been an uphill battle. My mother became pregnant with me at a very young age. By my teenage years, I had been confronted with the harsh realities of drug addiction, poverty, and homelessness. Survival was a daily struggle. Food was scarce, and each day was a challenge just to make it through. There were days, weeks, and months when I had no stable place to call home. During my high school years, I depended on free breakfasts and lunches, grateful for the warm roof over my head during the bitterly cold winter months.

Between our stretches of homelessness, I became pregnant. On June 5, 1990, at the age of 18, I graduated from

T.W. Josey High School located in my hometown of Augusta at nine months pregnant. Several weeks later, I gave birth to Jacques, my oldest son. Several months after the birth of my Jacques, we moved to River Glenn Housing Projects located in an area known by natives as "The Bottom." Jacques and I lived in River Glenn the first two and a half years of his life. While living there, I was unemployed and received Aid to Families with Dependent Children (AFDC – commonly known as Welfare) and supplemental assistance from the Women-Infant-Children (WIC) Program from the State of Georgia. Those years were filled with profound challenges as I struggled to balance the weight of young motherhood with the relentless cycles of poverty and uncertainty, all while trying to attend Augusta Technical College.

I realized that the best way for me to provide food, clothing, shelter, medical, and dental care for my son was for me to join one of the branches of the United States military. Three months prior to my 21st birthday, I gave temporary custody of Jacques to my beloved grandmother Mary and enlisted in the United States Army in the Military Occupational Specialty (MOS) of 74C – Radio Telecommunications Center Operator. My decision to enlist changed the entire trajectory of our lives.

By the age of 25, I was married. By the age of 26, while residing in Belgium, a beautiful European country, I gave birth to my youngest son, DeShon Jr. Then, by the age of 35, I was divorced. With years of experience and a job with benefits, I was able to withstand the impact of once again being a single parent, soldier, and college student. As I walked along the beach, I reflected on how I had embodied a unique blend of grit that ignited my *fire* throughout those difficult years.

As the single point of failure for my household, my focus remained unshakable because any misstep would have rippled through my children's lives. The balance between single parenthood and the heavy responsibilities of active-duty service seemed impossible at times, but I pressed on. The ocean breeze carried with it the weight of those memories, the daily victories of being both mother, soldier, and college student from organizing our busy schedules to raising my sons, while never losing sight of duty to my country.

The stillness of the night reminded me of the most difficult part of it all, the countless "Mommy will be back" and "Mommy will see you soon." It took immense courage to leave my children behind in our homeland, to fight in foreign countries, knowing each departure could be my last. The sound of the waves rolling in and out echoed the rhythm of my years spent in uniform, with each return home bittersweet as I had to prepare for the next time I would have to leave.

The life of *"soldier girl,"* like the ebb and flow of the ocean before me, was shaped by the fierce power of love, sacrifice, and duty. As I continued along the beach, I thanked God for the strength that carried me throughout my military career. My paygrade upon initial entry was Private, the lowest United States Army rank. Over the course of 26 years, one month and 12 days of active-duty military service, as a 74C, I achieved the ranks from Private (PV1) to Staff Sergeant (SSG). Then, once I transitioned from being an Enlisted Soldier to a Warrant Officer in the MOS of 254A – Signal Systems Support Technician and 255A – Information Services Technician, I achieved the ranks from Warrant Officer One (WO1) to Chief Warrant Officer Five (CW5). On November 26, 2018, I was medically retired from the United States Army in the rank of Chief Warrant Officer Five, the highest Warrant Officer rank within the United States Army.

Throughout this lengthy military career, my duty assignments allowed my children and I to reside in the United States, Asia, and Europe. Long after the fireworks had faded, the legacy of those moments remains forever imprinted in my heart as a reminder of the toll my military sacrifices took, not only on me but on my children as well. Despite many challenges, I enjoyed *becoming soldier girl.*

My military children suffered from PTSD, too!

As the calm of the evening settled, I reflected on my life since retirement. But, in doing so, I was sadly reminded of how my military service negatively impacted my children. Since I am no longer busy playing *"soldier girl,"* I have lots of time to reflect on my past sacrifices and decisions.

My children are now adult men, each forging their own paths in life. I lost *time* with my children during the most critical milestones of their childhood. *Time* that I can never get back.

But it's not just *time* that I lost, I screamed silently in my head. What about the mental state of my children, I shrieked out loud to no one in particular. I chuckled as I realized that my unexpected outburst resulted in a few confused and wide-eyed stares from several beach goers.

You see, throughout my military career, as a single parent, a dual-military parent, and then a single parent again, there were long stretches when I barely saw my children at all. Sometimes I did not see my children for weeks or months that teetered very close to a year. In my mind I erroneously assumed that I was the *"ONLY"* person making sacrifices while being away from my children. I never considered the impact my deployments had on my children. It never occurred to me that my children were emotionally distressed and periodically lived in environments where they felt unwelcome, unloved, and unsafe.

During periods of long separations from me, my children faced emotional challenges such as anxiety, fear, and loneliness. As I paused to look out at the darkness that covered the ocean, I recalled multiple overseas unaccompanied assignments to Korea that took me away from my children twice. The first time a 12-month tour and the second time an 18-month tour. During each of these tours, I only spent up to 30 days with my children. Then I recalled the 12-month deployments. During each deployment I returned home to my children to enjoy the allocated 14-day Rest & Relaxation (R&R).

Later I learned that my absence from their lives during critical developmental stages lead my children to feeling abandoned, confused, unloved, and insecure. But each time I returned home from an overseas unaccompanied assignment or military deployment, I was mentally exhausted from living and working in a high paced and stressful environment. Unfortunately, I was unable to emotionally reconnect with my children or manage my own stress effectively.

Looking back on my military career, I realize that my children suffered from PTSD too. The impact of PTSD within my children manifested in several ways. My numerous military assignments invaded my thoughts like an unwanted movie marathon. My children experienced *emotional distress* because they felt isolated, anxious, and fearful for my safety and theirs. I wiped the tears from my eyes as I recalled many years ago when Jacques said, "mommy when I was younger and you would go away for the Army, I thought you left me because you did not love me or want me." I was surprised and asked him what made him think such thoughts. He said, "Because everyone else has a mommy and their mommy was always at home with them. But my mommy was never home with me. So, I thought that you did not love me or want me." These words were very heartbreaking for me to hear. My reality was that while I was serving my country and earning my paycheck, my children not only struggled with the fear and anxiety of not knowing if I would ever return home to them, but also whether or not I loved them at all.

By the time the Global War On Terrorism was in full swing, Jacques was in high school and DeShon Jr. was in the 1st Grade. Although Jacques was one of the smartest kids in his class, he began to exhibit *behavioral changes*, became emotionally withdrawn, acted out and had difficulty concentrating. Sadly, during those days I had not been formally diagnosed with PTSD. Looking back, I realize that because of my rapid deployments I barely noticed or addressed the behavioral changes of my child until it was too late. My children were emotionally withdrawn because they felt repeatedly abandoned. Meanwhile, I struggled with irritability, emotional numbness, and detachment, which caused a **relationship strain** between me and my children. Perhaps me nor my children understood why I seemed distant or reactive. My behavior perhaps caused my children to feel confused or guilty. Unbeknownst to me, Jacques, who was just a child himself, felt unloved and was mistreated by those who were left in charge to care for him, often times found himself being overly protective of his little brother DeShon Jr. Because of my constant military assignments and deployments, with the disruption of their daily lives and sense of security, my oldest son **role reversed** and became prematurely mature in order to survive his unwanted and sometimes hostile living environments.

Meanwhile DeShon Jr. displayed his emotional traumas differently. As I reflect over the years, I realize that he did not express his emotions or cry. Instead, he focused his attention elsewhere. DeShon Jr. developed an addictive habit of playing video games and spent most of his free time at home either lost in the fantasy world of video games or lost in the fantasy world of his toys. Yet, DeShon Jr.'s biggest passion aside from video games was his love of sports. As one of the great, great nephews of the world heavyweight champion "Joe Louis" Barrow aka The Brown Bomber, it is no surprise that he participated in recreational and school sports such as wrestling, football, basketball, baseball, and track throughout his childhood.

Although DeShon Jr. played multiple sports from the age six until high school graduation, his trauma caused him to forget about his younger days of playing sports. As I walked along the beach and kicked sand under my feet, I recalled the conversation and moment that I realized that DeShon Jr. was perhaps mentally traumatized too. From 2011 – 2016, DeShon Jr. and I resided in Germany. When we arrived in Germany, he was an 8th Grader, he was a high school graduate headed to college when we departed. While DeShon Jr. was away at college I unpacked our family home. During his first visit back home from college after our home was finally unpacked and settled, he noticed unfamiliar things throughout his childhood bedroom. DeShon Jr. had no recollection of his childhood prior to the 8th grade. He actually said to me, "Ma, who's trophy's, certificates, pictures, awards and stuff are in my room?" I looked at him and said, "DeShon are you serious?" He replied, "yes!" I said, "DeShon, those are your accolades. Look at them. They all have your name and pics on them." My baby was so traumatized from his youth that he did not remember playing any sports or receiving awards and recognition during his school years from 1st to the beginning of his 8th Grade school years. This reality brought tears to my eyes because I was reminded that during this same timeframe, I deployed every other year. Which means I was never at home for an entire school year, with my children, only partial school years. Because either I was deployed or training and preparing for future deployments.

Ultimately, my trauma, combined with prolonged absences and unpredictable returns back home, created emotional ripples that affected my children throughout their childhood. My children had to bear the weight of these challenges, while trying to reconcile the changes in my behavior, and the prolonged absences caused by my military obligations.

Military life molds us into people who can handle high stress, pressure, and the demands of duty. But what we often overlook is how much our children bear the burden of that same life, and how military life impacts them as deeply as it does the service member. Now, I realize that early intervention and family focused support groups to provide stability for military families, not just the service member will help to mitigate PTSD among military children. Because *my military children suffered from PTSD too!*

Time

My military service profoundly shaped my children's lives. We made sacrifices that many will never fully understand. The *time* we lost together left wounds that no passage of *time* can heal. As I gazed at the rolling waves of the ocean, I reflected on how often people question my frequent vacation travels with my adult sons. The truth is, while others enjoyed the comfort of home with their loved ones, my children were often left in the care of relatives who didn't always prioritize their well-being. I missed too many milestone moments, and memories with my children when they needed me the most. Whether I was preparing for deployments, actively deployed, or on unaccompanied assignments, I was absent from their lives when my presence mattered most.

Life is fleeting, and *time* waits for no one. Those lost years with my children are forever etched in my mind, a constant reminder that the sacrifices they endured were just as heavy as my own. The weight of that absence is something I carry with me daily. The pain of missed moments lingers, but as long as God continues to bless me and my children with life, I will cherish every second I can spend with my two precious heartbeats.

I laugh now when I think of what I imagined retirement would be like. I thought family life would fall into place easily once I retired. I envisioned stronger family bonds, peace, and tranquility after years of living the fast-paced military life. But reality didn't match my expectations.

Instead, I find myself constantly feeling the need to apologize, to make up for the *time* I missed. My children are my **"WHY"** because they are the two most significant people in my life. So, when you see me and my heartbeats traveling the world to yet another exotic destination, understand that we are not just vacationing, we are reclaiming our precious and lost *time.*

From Soldier Girl to Veteran

After a delicious seafood dinner, I found myself back by the ocean. This time, instead of walking along the beach, I stood quietly, letting the sound of the waves and the salty breeze wash over me. In this stillness, I reflected on what it truly means to become a veteran. It is not just about stepping away from active duty; it's about embracing a profound shift in identity, purpose, and navigating life outside of the military. This transformation has been more than a change of uniform, it is the evolution of identity and bridging of two worlds. One world, where service, duty, and camaraderie were at the core of everything, and now a new world of personal growth, new beginnings, and a continued pursuit of purpose.

When I first joined the United States Army, becoming a veteran wasn't something I thought about because my main priority was escaping poverty. Now, as I stand by the ocean, I realize that this transition has been a slow, impactful process that has deeply touched not just me but also my children and family. Every gentle wave of the ocean reminds me of the challenges we've faced and the new path we are on together.

After serving over 26+ years of military training, deployments, and the relentless pressures of being a soldier, the time eventually came for me to transition into a new chapter. Transitioning from *soldier girl to veteran* has been more challenging and disorienting than I anticipated. Even in retirement, my mindset and expectations remain rooted in the military, where precision, discipline, and accountability were non-negotiable. Now, without the structure and clear sense of purpose that defined my military life, I often feel displaced, as if a piece of me is missing.

My expectations vs reality was a hard lesson learned. I imagined retirement as a relief, a new chapter of freedom, and a fresh start with my children. But the reality was very different. I quickly realized that the journey from *"soldier girl"* to veteran did not end with my last day in uniform. For many, the transition into retirement takes time and adjustment. Unfortunately, my transition was more abrupt, as I was medically retired, forcing me into a reality I wasn't fully prepared for.

The sudden change of my military status required me to be mentally, emotionally, and financially prepared.

Fortunately, I was able to utilize the ***Army Soldier for Life – Transition Assistance Program (SFL-TAP)***. Although I did not begin the SFL-TAP process during the recommended 18 to 24 months prior to retirement, I still significantly benefited from its services offered. SFL-TAP provided essential support as I transitioned from active duty to civilian life, offering a variety of workshops, services, and counseling. The program prepared me for the job market, guided me on making future career decisions, and educated me on veteran's benefits.

SFL-TAP played a fundamental role in ensuring I was equipped to face life after the military. It covered everything from resume writing, job search strategies to interviewing techniques and how to leverage the skills I developed throughout my Army career. Becoming a veteran was not the end of my story. Instead, it marked the beginning of a new chapter, one filled with opportunities to honor my past while embracing the future. Through it all, I carry with me the lessons learned, the bonds formed, and the resilience that defines the triumph of my journey *from soldier girl to veteran.*

Waves Of Transition

As I stood barefoot on the warm sand, feeling the cool ocean breeze, I reflected on how far I had come. The rhythmic crash of the waves was soothing, but my thoughts drifted to the challenges I faced while preparing for my unexpected medical retirement. I realized that transition begins long before your last day in uniform. It can take years, not just months, to mentally prepare and plan your next steps. The wind swirled around me as I thought about the importance of rebuilding a support system. Leaving the military meant losing the camaraderie of my fellow soldiers and our irreplaceable bond. Thankfully, I found organizations that help service members transition into civilian life. Ultimately, what got me through my transition was igniting every element of my *fire* and knowing I was not alone. Though the uniforms have been packed away, **"soldier girl"** remains within me. My skills in self-discipline, problem-solving, and perseverance continue to help me navigate the challenges of civilian life.

For those preparing to transition, be proactive. Do not wait until the last minute to plan your next move. It is important to start transitioning early. Understand that reality might not match expectations. Take advantage of the available resources and information and know that asking for help is a sign of strength. Build a new support system. Face mental health head-on. Take time to adjust to the new normal. Redefine purpose and passion. Take care of finances. Never stop reaching out. You've already proven your resilience in service to our country. Now apply that same strength to building a fulfilling life after retirement. My fellow veterans, you've got this. Now, enjoy *your waves of transition.*

We Are Veterans

Later that night, as I sat by the ocean, the quiet stillness enveloped me. The rhythmic crashing of the waves provided the perfect backdrop for my thoughts. I am a parent, daughter, sister, cousin, friend, and **Soldier For Life.** November holds a special significance in my heart, not just because it marks my retirement after 26+ years of active-duty military service, but because it is a month dedicated to honoring my fellow Veterans. This time of reflection reminds me of the transformation from soldier to Veteran and the enduring bond I share with my brothers and sisters in arms, my Battle Buddies.

In these reflective moments, I feel immense pride and honor for having served alongside such remarkable men and women, in both peace and war. To my fellow Veterans, you hold a special place in my heart that words can hardly capture. Your unwavering dedication, sacrifice, and service represent the core values I live by every day. I am privileged to have shared this journey with you. The acronym I created for Veterans symbolizes my admiration for your commitment, capturing the essence of who you are and the legacy you continue to uphold. *We are Veterans.*

VALOR: Infused in every step of the way. Your courage and bravery are woven into the very fabric of your service.

ENDURING: Unwavering resilience, unbroken spirit. You have faced every challenge with steadfast resolve, never wavering in your commitment.

TENACITY: Beyond boundaries and despite obstacles. Your relentless determination has allowed you to overcome even the greatest hardships.

EXEMPLIFYING: Honor and sacrifice. You set the highest standards through your honorable service, putting the needs of others before your own.

RESPECTED: Guardians, standing tall. You are the protectors of freedom, standing tall with pride and respect for the values you defend.

ADMIRABLE: Selfless service to country, bravery. Your willingness to serve selflessly, with courage and strength, inspires all who know your story.

NOBLE HEARTS: United and strong. Together, as one, you embody the heart and soul of our nation's resilience and spirit.

STEADFAST PATRIOTS: Defenders of liberty. You remain unwavering in your defense of the liberty and freedoms that define our great country.

Thank you for your service. God Bless You, and God Bless America.

"I can do all things through Christ which strengthens me."

KJV Philippians 4:13

*"You are **fearless**, **inspired**, **resilient**, and **empowered** because you have survived the many obstacles thrown in your path. Embrace your strength of a warrior and refuse to give up hope."*
~ Sonya Howell Barrow

DR. SONYA HOWELL BARROW

ARMY

CHIEF WARRANT OFFICER FIVE (CW5)

Contact Sonya:

EMAIL: hello@sonyahowellbarrow.com

WEBSITE: http://www.sonyahowellbarrow.com

LINKTREE: https://linktr.ee/sonyahowellbarrow

FACEBOOK: https://www.facebook.com/authorpreneursonya

INSTAGRAM: https://www.instagram.com/authorpreneursonya

LINKEDIN: https://www.linkedin.com/in/sonyahowellbarrow/

AMAZON AUTHOR CENTRAL:
https://www.amazon.com/stores/Sonya-Howell-Barrow/author/B0C5425D8W?

THE STORY OF VETERAN

MICHAEL SEAN CHRISTIAN KELLEY

My name is Michael Sean Christian Kelley. I have worn many titles as well as been called by 3 of my 4 names so it can be quite confusing to who I really am. I have had a hard time remembering some of the titles as well as names :) I grew up as Sean. I then joined the military where I was Kelley. Though a lot of my friends as we were the "rough broken family posse" (because most of us were poor and came from broken homes with drugs and alcohol at the forefront) most of my friends called me Kelley as well. I then began working in the "real world " (as I call it) and became Michael. Then we get to the "titles". I have been Mr. Kelley as I am a schoolteacher. I have also been known as SSG Kelley, which I will explain in this chapter. I also was once known as a husband, but the title that I hold nearest and dearest to my heart is Dad.

So, coming from a broken home and doing what most who come from backgrounds that involve instability tend to do. We gravitate to the things in life that help you escape. Mine began as sports. I never quite felt comfortable in sports as it was competitive, and I wasn't real keen on losing. Nor did I feel like financially I belonged since most of the kids on the teams I was on had "parents" (plural) and nice homes with nice things. I, on the other hand, quite the opposite. I then turned my back on sports and found music, which played (literally) a MAJOR role in my transfer from youth to adult. I played guitar very well and played in some of my area's hottest bands. We packed bars and signed autographs as though we were famous. We partied hard and rocked even harder. That would be a whole other book, so let's cut it off there. Some of my music can still be found on YouTube. Under "THE WARDOG UNDERGROUND".

Now, being poor took me from sports, but I fit right in on the music scene as most musicians are tormented souls from crap background. That is not to say that I did not have family members step in to keep us afloat and make my youth somewhat bearable. I give props to Billy and

Madonna Bell Edington my grandparents on my mother's side as well as a Great Aunt and Uncle William "Weep" and Freda Searing. Without those individuals we would have been on the streets or in much less desirable circumstances. I want to shout out to my mother Donna Ruth Kelley/Walter for doing her best with the hand she was dealt with raising me and my oldest sister. Okay now that the intro is over lol. Let's begin Pfft.

I SSG Kelley did 21 yrs in the United States Army. I was what they call a "lifer", meaning I made a career out of the military. I was a 19K38K8. I know that doesn't mean a lot to a civilian but let me translate. I was a M1A1 Abrams Tank Crewman (at one time holding all positions Driver, Loader, Gunner, Tank Commander). I was also an Instructor as well as a Tank Master Gunner, holding the rank of SSG E-6. I have been stationed CONUS as well as OCONUS (United States and Overseas). I have been deployed as a security force for the 1996 Olympics Atlanta, GA, to SFOR 9 Bosnia Herzegovina, and OIF 1-2 (Operation Iraqi Freedom). I am affiliated with the 12th CAV REG from my time serving with 1-12 CAV 1st CAV DIV. I wear 1 foreign award. The German Armed Proficiency Badge (Silver). I am a "Spur" and "Buckle" holder. My highest award earned was the Meritorious Service Medal. I was not a hero; I was a soldier who did my job above the normal standard, which is why I am a Master Gunner.

As a Master Gunner, I got to do some things out of the normal box. I got lucky and got an assignment with the AGR (Active Guard or Reserves) program. I was the State "Mike Golf" (as we are called) at a National Guard base. I got to go to Sniper School with the local law enforcement academy to help set up and monitor their ranges. I also got to go to CQB, Master Breacher, and 13B (Field Artillery) Course as well. Yes, I am a "Red Leg" as well as a Tank Mike Golf. So, during my career in the military, I was fortunate enough to have a pretty solid foundation at home. I was married and entered the military with two children which then turned into many years of service and four children.

The main reason for staying was my children. My oldest son was born with some medical issues that would have broken me as a civilian. The military provides excellent health insurance as well as educational opportunities for our dependents, aka children, etc. Now, I knew that one day I would retire from the military and go back into the civilian world, and I looked so forward to it.

I had so many dreams. I had 3 major ones. The main reason for some of my dreams was to secure my children, now young adults in this life. I wanted a motorcycle shop, and a Brewery, which I eventually turned my focus into a coffee shop. I just figured as much as I promote riding a motorcycle that I didn't need to align it with drinking and riding. So, being a combat veteran as well as a career soldier, we are trained to work hard and play hard. It's no secret that we in the military tend to drink a little here and there. That's another chapter that's another book HOOAH.

Well, I, being a former rock star in the most Unfamous Famous band on earth, took that to heart. I began a long-lasting relationship with the "drink". So, here I am knee-deep in a military career. We were stationed in Sunny SoCal, and I was about to get promoted to SFC E-7 (within 2 weeks). We had waited 1 year to move into "Senior" housing and were 1 week out from that. I was sitting in my garage having a beverage, and my wife then walked in and said, and I quote, "I'm DONE".

Now, mind you 20, 20-plus years of marriage, I have heard it time and time again. However, there was something different this time. I was not only in shock, but my whole world was about to crumble and, to this day, NEVER be the same. Everything we / I had built was on the line. I began the whole begging process, then, please forgive me (even though she was not perfect by no means). I tried to humble myself, and the more I tried, the further my former life as I knew it was slipping away. Into the depths of what would become my "new norm".

So here we are today ... Divorced (surprise), my four beautiful children Sierra, Liam, Conor, and Saige, aka "Jude," do their best to avoid me and cut me essentially out of their lives. Now, I do not blame the children as much as I blame the situation. I retired medically from the US Army in 2018. Since then, I started and lost a wonderful career, went through a shit fuck of a divorce which I lost pretty much everything I had worked for in my life up to that point. I lost all close ties with my children due to the extensive arguing and pissing off my now ex. Though she says, it has "nothing" to do with that, it was "all" my drinking (which was excessive at times, and yes, there were some serious issues legally and others). However, a good lawyer will break you in 30 different languages. Hers was so good I have sent multiple people to her. She took not only my money but half of my soul.

When I was first alerted that "she" was "done,." We were in California. We are Hoosier Indiana Cornbread born, so it was here that she chose to come back to with our kids at the time. I was so devastated and crippled as I was in a horrible mindset that I just resigned my AGR tour with 17 Active Duty Years and 2 weeks from promotion. I couldn't go on any further without them. They were my rocks and my reasons for getting up and putting up with some of the dumbshit the military has to offer.

We came back to Indiana. She got a house with the kids and without me. My purpose here isn't to beat anyone down. Just tell my story. Am I perfect? NO, I am NOT... However, nor is anyone else HOOAH. Anyway, enough about that. So, she and the kids are safe and sound. I am still helping pay the bills as she worked as well. However, the diff was I got to sleep in my truck at rest stops and surf couches and stay in shady hotels while they were safe and sound. I was glad my kids were protected. I was extremely pissed at her for LEAVING ME IN THE COLD. She will NEVER know the impact and devastation that did to me. Now again this isn't a bash, folks. I'm not better I am as fkd up as they come. However, I TOOK MINE ON THE CHIN.

So, I was LOST. I went from the Readiness NCO, Training NCO, and Master Gunner for an Armor Unit in California to a jobless, broken, reliant on alcohol to cope, and a just lost man. My first thought was get into school. Go finish your welding degree and teach. I went to a local college and did exactly that. I signed up for school. They put me in touch with the Dept. Chair and he found out I wanted to teach and was an Instructor in the Army and hired me on the spot. So now I am a schoolteacher, and my life was on the up and up professionally. However, my personal life was about to sink further and further into the void.

Somehow or another due to other imperfections, I ended up under the same roof as my ex and my children. We moved from that place her dad set her and our children up in a Log Cabin in the woods. Seemed as though things were on the mend. Well without going into great detail alcohol showed its dark light upon thee and, wala, I was homeless again. It's funny when you fall down how those who are equally as worthless try and point out your flaws so as to "pass the buck". Either way blah blah fkn blah blah. So now, I'm staying in my truck again and teaching school. Mind you I wasn't staying in my truck due to lack of resources and or funds. I was staying in my truck because I was just broken. I was so lost without my family. The very people that gave me purpose. The holidays were coming up and I did not know what to expect. Well, I somehow ended up back in the house. It seemed as though some things were being mended. I felt like I was on pins and needles.

We made a choice to move to my dad's old house on the lake. Painted Hills Lake which is a magical place, and it was actually where me and my ex and children began our journey once we got serious about our relationship. So now we have a house (that she CANNOT kick me out of since my dad owns it lol). We were doing great, working and putting our broken lives post military back together.

Then my ex gets an itch to vacate Indiana. The very state we just abandoned our lives in Sunny SoCal for. So, she gets an opportunity in Texas where we were once stationed. Our 2 oldest kids were going to stay here in an apt and go to college while her and our youngest children would move to TX with her, and I would stay and finish my contract with the place I taught College Welding to. We put all of our stuff in storage, and I moved her and the 2 youngest to an apt that her facility she worked for paid for. It was a nice place, and the kids seemed to love living in TX for the time being anyway.

As my contract neared its end I was offered a full-time teaching job with this college. When I told my ex about it, she said to take it. Because that way if TX didn't work out she could come back to IN. I didn't care where I just wanted my family back together.

Skipping past some of life's events we ended up back in IN. The year 2018 was a great year for our family. Myself, my ex and my oldest daughter all graduated from college. My oldest son graduated from High School, and my youngest children, well, I am not sure, but they were along for the ride, and they both rule earth. HOOAH. Me, my ex, and my oldest actually got good paying jobs as well. Great Year.

We soon after bought a home. Mind you, this was the 2nd home we ever bought. We lost our first one in a flood (that is another book as well). Some say that the loss of our first home is where we went south as a family unit. So here we are, brand new home, good jobs, and poof. She finally filed for divorce after all these years of struggle. Well, alcohol, fights, distance, careers, ALL of it took its toll, and we just couldn't go on.

So begins my New Norm. I went from an apartment to a Brand-New Toy Hauler. By this point, I am so damn tired of being kicked out of MY / OUR homes that I could just puke. So, I bought this toy hauler and moved it to a nice quiet campground and began the loneliest 2 and 1/2 years of my life. I never knew silence could be so loud. Well, it can. I drank and drank and mourned and felt so isolated and alone. By this time, my kids had all but given up on me. It was them against me. What a fkn letdown. I worked my whole life to facilitate the people I love. Now again this is my side and the events how I see them.

During this mourning process I tried to go out with a few ladies here and there and kept very close contact with some on the net through social media as most do this day of age. In the end, it is all just passing time, and it can be very unhealthy as well as cause muchos grande trouble. I just spent so much time doing stuff that I never in a million years would have been doing had I been back with the very people I loved the most in this life. Riding Harleys, Drinking, Skirmishes, Cruising around, coping the only way I didn't know how.

Then, one day, BOOM. I found myself huddled over in the shower, dry heaving while trying to pour whiskey down my throat and doing so until I quit dry heaving. It was time for change. I stayed with a female friend. One that I didn't have, nor did she have a love interest in. Somebody who knew the Real Sean Kelley from way back in the day and from way back home. Tabbi, YOU don't even know how much you helped me by letting me sleep on that so comfy couch. I needed that break from work and ALL of IT.

I began going to the VA and got myself completely squared away. I am a disabled combat Veteran, and that is that. I needed to get done what I got done. That helped secure my now future and what I am aiming towards at this time. I worked briefly with Harley Davidson (Thank You, Eric, Lori, Andrew, and Fro). They even sent me to Milwaukee for HD Academy, the first actual class of its kind. I got to ride my HD to the Mecca of HD. Junea Ave at the original factory. I was in HOG Heaven (literally). I even hit a car on my HD riding back from Milwaukee in Chicago rush hour traffic.

I was going pretty fast and slammed into the rear of a stopped car. Cracked some ribs and left a dent in the trunk with my ass. Could a been way worse. Totaled my bike. However. I got a new one... Speaking of, during this time, I cleaned my apt up and quit looking for love and left all those ladies alone HOOAH.

That's when "she" called. It was Memorial Day, and I was sitting there alone and just kind of well buzzed. The phone rings. I answered and it was a lady of whom I have had some previous history with. Mainly friends. However, friends that talk about anything and everything. She herself has suffered tremendous loss and went through a divorce after 25 yrs herself. So, we had a lot in common. She called to check on me like a friend check. I just felt compelled to tell her to come over. Reluctantly, she did. She knew where we both were and knew it could be dangerous. Oh man, was it, lol. If danger was a love story this mfkn night was DANGER RANGER in the dark BEING VERY DANGEROUS without his seatbelt on for sure. WOW. I was floored by how beautiful and sensual this woman was. I hadn't felt that kind of intensity since I said "I Do" years and another lifetime ago.

This was the turning point for all things Sean. As I began to pick up my Broken pieces and put them together. I was falling in LOVE fast and furious. ALL I wanted was to be in the presence of this wonderful, amazing, beautiful, smart, woman. I have lived many lives. Once as a soldier. People It's Gets Better. No, it doesn't not. LMAO. I am so sorry I seen that on FB and it still makes me laugh.

People, THERE IS LIGHT at the end of the Tunnel. In the darkest of dark. Please, please know that somewhere somehow, LIGHT WILL shine through. I am on the mend.

I want to close this chapter with this. I am a prime example of being cast out. However, I am casting myself back in. I have a beautiful friend. I have 4 wonderful kids who are now young adults. I have a family that I am repairing relations with. I have some littles in the mix now as well. I have a beautiful granddaughter, and my nephews are not only my little buddies, but they are riding little dirt bikes YAY :) I have a wonderful job teaching welding again. I am an example of a shit show that fell completely apart. Just grind the edges. Bevel them suckers and weld them back together. Michael Sean Christian Kelley Forever, Forever Michael Sean Christian Kelley Hooah

MICHAEL SEAN CHRISTIAN KELLEY

ARMY

MEDICALLY RETIRED AS A SSG E-6

THE STORY OF VETERAN

JON COX

I graduated high school and decided, like most new adults, I would go to college. I was not ready! After one wasted year and $9,000 in student loan debt, I found myself in a factory working for $7.00 an hour at 19 years old. I was immature and had no direction. One year later my older brother who 7 years earlier had joined the Navy, had returned from his duty station in Spain to become a Navy recruiter. I was not close to him at the time due to our age difference and the fact that he had been in Spain for the past 5 years. He had shown up with his new Spanish wife to stay with us in a 2-bedroom trailer. His intention was to buy a house but that would take at least a month. Once I had seen his house, helped him move in, and witnessed his lifestyle, I was sold! I was going to be a Sailor! The following week, I took a day off from the factory, walked into his recruiting office and said, "Put me in brother!"

I joined the Navy in February of 1994! I was initially an Intelligence Specialist and assigned to the USS John C. Stennis (CVN-74) the newest Aircraft carrier prior to its commissioning. I ended up becoming a plank owner and left there to report to recruiting in February 1998 in Indianapolis, Indiana. Following this duty station, I was assigned to a recruiting station in Akron, Ohio to run a station from 2002-2005, where I ended up making Chief Petty Officer. After Akron, I transferred to Cincinnati, Ohio to run my first division from 2005-2008. From there I was assigned to go work for the Recruiting Training and Inspection Team in Millington, Tennessee at CNRC in 2008. While there, I made Senior Chief in 2009, and in 2010 I received Individual Augmentee orders to Afghanistan for a year to help recruiting efforts for the Afghan Army to help fill all medical units in the country. Upon my return to CNRC, I was made Master Chief in 2012 and transferred to Minneapolis, Minnesota in 2013. I was then transferred to San Antonio, Texas in 2015 and then back to Minneapolis in 2017. I retired on February 28, 2018, after 24 years of service.

Throughout my military career, a few of my biggest highlights included accomplishing Intelligence Specialist "A" School in Dam Neck, Virginia. I had never worked so hard on applying myself in an educational manner, which is when I learned how to have a work/life balance, and I have the Navy to thank for that. Writing my first contract as a Navy Recruiter was the best feeling ever, and I will never forget their name. In 2004, getting pinned to Chief Petty Officer was a moment that I had wanted since I went to "A" school. One week after I was pinned to Senior Chief in 2009, my brother and mentor, Chief Petty Officer Cox retired from the Navy after 24 years of service in Virginia and I was able to be there, outranking him, lol. In 2012, after my yearlong deployment in Afghanistan, I found out I had made Master Chief, and this was quite rewarding for my family as they had made many sacrifices during my entire career, and at that point, I had accomplished something that we never even imagined.

Going into retirement or transition, every senior leader puts on a smile and says, "I'm good." On the inside we are all scared as hell. I thought with my skills and experience, I would have companies fighting over Master Chief Cox to come lead any team in their company and pay me two to three times the salary I was making in the military. While serving, my fellow sailors and I would often discuss how many hours we work and how much we are worth on the outside. I was thinking, "I am going to be rich and work much less than I did in the military." Reality hit fast and hard! I was about one year out from retirement and decided to drop my papers to announce my intention to retire. I completed my resume, looked at what my retirement pay would be for an E-9 with 24 years, and started going to my medical appointments when I had the time. I still had to work at my command, and I felt ahead of the game. I was wrong by a long shot and had no idea. My retirement check was going to be 60% of my base salary, which means no more tax-free housing allowance, food allowance, special duty pay, or clothing allowance which is included in active duty pay. I was taking a huge pay cut and did not know anything about the VA benefits. My command allowed me to sign up for one transition class at Great Lakes Naval Base in Illinois and I scheduled it 9 months prior to my retirement date. I had three months until that class. I felt like I should start attending career fairs and sending out resumes.

I attended my first career fair within a few weeks of signing up for that transition class, with my resume and my 20 years of recruiting experience. I walked in confident and cocky, but sadly walked out confused and frustrated. I had spoken to every table in there. I was no longer recognized as the Master Chief when I entered the room, I was just another person. That took a little time to sink in. I was either overqualified or not qualified enough for the jobs they had, or my start date was too far out for the job they needed to fill now and so on. When a few of the employers asked me how much I was looking to get paid, I paused as it was a tricky question to answer at a career fair. With 40% of my income disappearing, plus the tax-free income that my family had gotten used to getting monthly, I knew I needed at least $60,000 a year to keep the same lifestyle. In my mind, I also knew my worth from all the conversations I had with my fellow military brothers and sisters. My answer to their salary question ended up being $150,000. Their response was "Good luck." Of course, I left with several business cards, and I had given out all 150 copies of my resume that day. I did not receive one phone call after that, and I was expecting my phone to ring non-stop, it did not. My pride was hurt, this is where most give up! Not Master Chief, not Jon from the trailer park raised by a single mother who grew up with just enough to survive, but we did!

If I learned anything from military recruiting it was, do not wait for them to make the decisions and call you, go after them. That is exactly what I did. I was going to get a job that took care of my family's needs and go from there. I started looking for regular recruiting jobs instead of recruiting director positions. I figured if they would not call me back when I applied for their leadership positions, would they call me when I applied for their experience required positions? Yes, they did, I started to get interviews. This opened my eyes to the fact that some people are lucky enough to walk right into a great position, that they always wanted, but if it is not the best position you still have to pay your bills and provide food on the table. I needed a job in a specific area, and I was not too proud to show a company what I was made of to start at a level lower than my current position.

In my mind, survival mode hit. I had to have a job; this is the recruiting mindset instilled in my twenty years' experience of making goals now! I started applying for jobs, building my LinkedIn, and connecting with recruiting jobs and recruiting professionals. In hindsight, I had focused my vision on recruiting in a smaller area, which limited my search. But what I needed was to open my search options and think about different career fields with my experience. The military gives you a wide variety of experiences that can translate to many jobs and position avenues in the civilian world. I started building my social media, especially LinkedIn, and connected with companies that I was interested in potentially working for. Once I started targeting positions that I did not necessarily see myself getting started in, lowering my expectations a little, I started getting interviews. This was a hard pill to swallow because it was below my skill level. I was retiring from the Navy as an E-9, with a bachelor's degree, and over 20 years of experience in the field I was applying for. Also, I had 15 years of leadership experience in that field. I was a top tier candidate. And looking back after recruiting for a corporate company I realize we looked internally first, because that is what we trusted. As we went external with all the HR fears and what you could not check as far as references and such it was hard to accept experiences all the time. Plus, I see how competitive of a market it is for high end corporate jobs, we received hundreds if not thousands of resumes for these high-end positions.

Interviews went well, I dressed to impress and was professional with none of that sailor vulgarity. I left the military lingo out of the conversations and just used common sense to answer their Human Resources questions. I kept my answers short and relevant to the question. I did my research on who I knew was going to be interviewing me prior to showing up, and on the history of the company and its leadership. I had a job offer within a few weeks of my first interview. My first job offer came in at $80,000 annually which was $20,000 more than I needed to cover what I was losing from retiring once I started receiving my retirement check. I did counteroffer to try to get a little more from my experience and ended up at $85,000. I did the counteroffer to try to increase my potential profit, however I would not always recommend this as it could backfire and lose you the position overall. I figured I would be making $25,000 more than I was making on active duty and I had not yet submitted my VA claim. That VA claim was potential for more money per month, and I was awaiting my transition class, which was in one month from then, and that is where I would get more information about the VA claim process. I accepted the position ten months prior to my retirement date and the company was willing to wait for me! It was a recruiting position, not in leadership, but there was room for growth. I was happy with the company's culture and looking back it was a smart choice. Being happy is an important part of the decision when picking your job when transitioning, which can prevent you from having multiple jobs in a short amount of time.

I attended the transition class a month later and for me, it was not worth the hype they had made it out to be. The instructors were prior military, who had come straight from retirement to teaching these transition classes. They had never experienced the civilian world and were unable to give good advice. They had told us not to settle for the lower end of the pay scale, to hold out for the jobs that had higher pay that were more than worth it. That is not always good advice if you have bills to pay or must put food on the table, which most people do. To me it was easy for them to tell all of us that we should do something to put our livelihood and families in jeopardy as they never had to experience the same thing. They walked right from active duty and crossed the street from one building to the next building changing from uniform to civilian clothes. They even bragged about how they started while they were on separation leave collecting both military pay and civilian pay. The VA record review was fast and not informative at all. The VA rep came in, gave a 30-minute speech, took each of our records and two days later gave it back with a post it notes on what to discuss with the Veterans Service office when you retire. I left that session more confused than when I had arrived. Their resume review was not up to date and, as a recruiter, needed to be up to the current industry standards. I was extremely disappointed with my experience! I did not like the fact that all of us service members had given 20 plus years of service to our country, which is a huge investment, and their return seemed like a discount or value meal. They should do better. It motivated me to show those two so called instructors up one day! Guess what I did, or so I believe!

Once it is all over, you take the cloth of the country off, you are no longer the wealth of knowledge, the go to person, the "Master Chief." All that 24 years is shoved into a shadowbox that gathers dust on a shelf that I look at often honestly, as it brings back great memories. Leaving all that was quite difficult for a long time. I was very depressed and "Woe is me," for the first few months. My phone stopped ringing; the Navy moved on and "Yes," it did fine without Master Chief Cox. I was having a challenging time finding out who I was now as my civilian self. Afterall, I had been in the Navy for 24 years and it made me who I was as a person. I found out fast that the struggle is real, the VA helped me with this. I had spent a year in Afghanistan in some stressful environments, so I did use their services to help me cope with PTSD, as it also helped me with my transition to civilian life also. I will also credit my family for helping and understanding what I was going through during this transition, they were a tremendous help. Communication with them and my VA doctors got me through those times and where I am today.

You have to find your purpose again! It was like I was that junior sailor again at my new job. I told myself "I did it before, I can do it again." I am sure we all heard it before, "get back to the basics." Guess what, just like any good veteran, I did. I showed my co-workers and my company what 24 years of military service and training can bring. I started as a recruiter, and within a year, I was asked to build a recruiting team and promoted to Director of Recruiting, a stockholder position of a 13-billion-dollar company with over 85,000 employees. I stayed away from those that told me things that could not happen or could not be done. I did them and made them happen, plus I showed others how to do those things. I jumped in to help others and tried to be a team player. Going against what they told me at the transition program had put me ahead of my peers from that program, along with most of my peers that had retired around the same time as me that knew.

I left this position in October 2023 after six years with the company. I have connections with them as I recommended my replacement who is running the recruiting department today. I left to spend more time with my wife and my children who are grown, and my son is in the Navy and my daughter is married to a sailor. Since I never want to stop, I have started doing my own podcast on recruiting to help spread my knowledge on best recruiting practices. I have also recently accepted a contractor position with a company as a facilitator for Navy Recruiter's teaching sales skills as Director Sales Effectiveness. This is more of a part time on my time position that allows me to be part of the organization that I love, plus help Navy recruiters be successful! I know if you believe in something you can sell it, I do believe in the Navy, I have a son and a son-in-law currently serving active duty and both deployed. I know the benefits of serving and what a military career can do for you, especially if you put your all into taking advantage of every situation even the times that are not so great.

I learned to be successful, not being in the Navy. I was taught to be successful by those I had served with, all the great leaders and even the not-so-great ones, as well. I learned from all the people I had served with, during the most challenging times of my life, even the times when we were unsure whether we would make it through it or not, but together we did! That is success, I just get up every day and do my best, help others get better, and when I fail at something, and I do, I get right back at it! I never let others dictate what I can or cannot accomplish, or what our company can or cannot accomplish. At some point, you must make decisions, do not wait for someone to tell you, it is okay for you to make decisions now! No one is going to do it for you, you must figure it out now.

When it comes to Transitioning from the military, I hope you can remember a few things from me. While you were active duty it was always about your people first, in transition it should be about you first. You must start early and make sure you have a solid plan to make it successful for you. Everyone will tell you what you should do, but no one will do anything for you. You must be the leader for yourself. Make your plan, stick to it, and hold yourself accountable! Be the subject matter expert, use those that have left before you, research before it sneaks up on you and be prepared. The more prepared you are the better chances you have of getting better results. I would hope in the future, especially for retirees, that the military would start a transition program that could happen 5 years before a retirement date. This could help reality sync in for some to see where they stand for preparedness, plus start a roadmap on what needs to happen in their last five years, or do they need to stay longer to obtain more to be competitive when they transition.

JON COX (WITH WIFE ANGIE)

NAVY

MASTERCHIEF PETTY OFFICER E-9

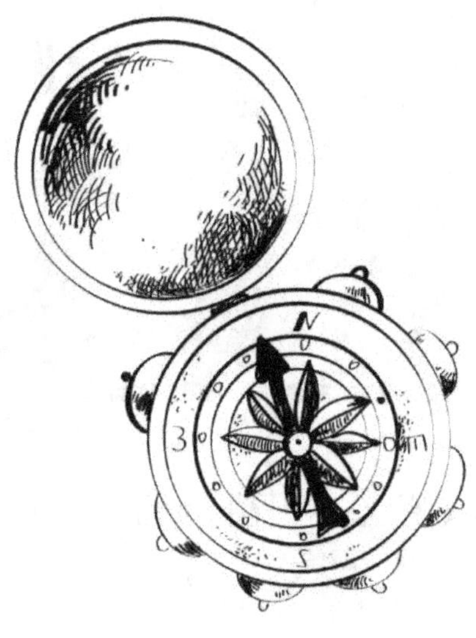

THE STORY OF VETERAN

ALICIA NOLAN

A SOLDIER'S FIGHT: BREAKING BARRIERS, FINDING STRENGTH

When I tell people I'm from Virginia Beach, VA, they assume that I came from a Navy family or at least a military family. I, in fact, did not come from a military family other than a grandfather who I didn't know well and an aunt who I also did not know very well. I knew nothing about the military other than what it was portrayed in commercials, TV shows, and movies. I didn't even know anyone who was in the military at the time.

When I graduated high school, I started working full-time and taking college classes here and there. Coming from a line of alcoholism, that's what my early twenties looked like. I worked, and I partied hard. At 25 years old, I finally felt like I needed to do something more. There was a fire in me that suddenly ignited into this desire to do something bigger with my life. I don't know where it came from, but it hit me hard. I felt like I had the discipline, physical strength, and mental strength to do something as hard as the military, or at least what I thought the military was going to be. I was right about a lot of my thoughts about joining the military, but I was very wrong about others.

Transitioning to the military life was an interesting experience. Again, I felt like I was made for the military or what I perceived the military to be. The beginning stages of my career were quite eye-opening, starting with basic training. I won't spoil it for you, but I will say that I had no issues getting through basic training. I tried not to be the best at tasks, but I certainly wasn't the worst at anything. I was athletic and stayed quiet. The drill sergeants left me alone, and if there is any advice I can give anyone going into the military, that was the perfect scenario. Advanced Individual Training (AIT) was the next phase. This experience was a little different for me.

AIT is where you go to learn your job in the military after basic training. I was 25 at the time, which meant I was one of the older individuals in that phase of training. Most soldiers were in their late teens and early twenties. Being who I am, I stuck to the rules and did what I was told. But I observed quite the rebellion from the younger soldiers. You'd think the instructors or senior leadership would get involved and straighten up those soldiers, but that was not the case. I did not understand it, and it started to confirm that I thought the military was not what I expected it to be.

The upside to being a "squared away" soldier was that I was usually offered more opportunities. For someone like me who is always trying to work to get to that next level, I felt perfect for the Army because it afforded many opportunities. The only thing that was incredibly tricky was the fact that I'm gay. And Don't Ask, Don't Tell (DADT) was still active when I joined. This was tricky to navigate because there was an appearance from most soldiers that they did not care about gay people being in the military, but you never knew who would care. I was very careful about who I opened myself up to and told.

After AIT, I went to airborne school. Yes, I volunteered to jump out of "perfectly good" airplanes. And I'm so glad I did because it was the start of a long, rewarding career in special forces. Because of airborne school, I was stationed at 10th Special Forces Group Airborne in Colorado Springs, Colorado, instead of Korea, where most of my class from AIT went. It was like a dream to be stationed there, and I knew how lucky I was. But here we are; DADT was still in full effect, and I needed to hop back into the closet because I just did not know who I was going to be working with.

At the beginning of my special operations career, I did satellite communications with a support company. I was good at it, and I loved being a soldier. I'm naturally an overachiever, and I never said no to any opportunity that I was offered. As I continued to excel in the position I was in, word spread around my unit about my work ethic, and I was given the opportunity of a lifetime: to work with a special company that worked in more clandestine environments. I did not know what this meant at the time, but the second I was told it would be great for my career, you did not have to say anything else. I said yes, and once again, I was on a new and exciting journey.

Once again, I found myself having to hide who I was just in case someone did not like the fact that I was gay. What is interesting is that shortly after this move, DADT was rightfully repealed, and I did not have to worry about being discharged from the Army for being gay. But I still felt like I had to hide who I was in the event that I would be discriminated against or treated differently. This was something I always had to consider and keep in the back of my mind no matter where I went.

In 2013, I had yet another opportunity fall into my lap. We had a new operations manager in the company, and he asked me if I wanted to go to free fall, scuba school, and others. Naturally, I said, yes. Who wouldn't say yes to all of that? What I was actually being offered was to be the guinea pig female for special forces. This was a huge role to take on, but I certainly would rather do it than allow any other female. I wanted to pave the way. But I had a lot to prove to all the male green berets, and I knew that. I was happy to take on that role, knowing there would be some challenges.

My mentor during this program was a highly respected green beret who had been in special forces for nearly twenty years. I looked up to him like he was my brother. He believed in the female program which is what really motivated me to perform to my best. I remember that moment when I knew I needed to come out to him because of some life events that were taking place at the time that your leadership should know about. I came out to him, and his response was, "Despite my religious convictions, you're still my soldier." At the time, I was not sure how to interpret that, but I also did not let it deter me from what I was doing. My thought was okay; he wants to be impartial, and even though he does not agree with me being gay, he would not use that against me in a professional capacity. And he never did.

I still did not come out of the closet openly until, one day, I had a revelation. But this revelation did not necessarily come willingly. I had to go up to my battalion command sergeant major for a meeting since I was technically still being interviewed to be the first female in special forces. As he was going through my enlisted record brief, he saw that I was married and asked about my husband. I did not correct him, and I played along. It ate away at me that night. I lost sleep over lying to my command sergeant major and decided that not only did I need to go to him the next day to tell him the truth, but I did not want to have to feel like I had to lie again.

I went to command sergeant major the next day and told him that I was married to a woman. Though at first, he seemed to be upset that I had lied to him, he also understood, and everything was okay. From that day forward, when someone asked me about my husband, I immediately corrected them and told them about my wife, and it was the most liberating feeling on the planet. My thought process was that if I did not make it weird, it was not weird, and it worked. The guys that I worked with genuinely did not care that I was gay if I could perform. Because, in all honesty, who cares who you sleep with as long as you can pull your own weight, show up, and be the best soldier you can be? That is literally all that matters.

I do have to share that one of the best things about being a gay woman and being the first in special forces was that one of the concerns across special forces was women sleeping with men. Clearly, that was not a concern of mine, but it did not stop rumors from happening. Of course, when I heard about the rumors, the only thing I could do was laugh. I feel like I was the best first female for such a program because I am gay. There were mixed feelings about females in special forces for various reasons, and I planned to make sure that none of those reasons came to fruition if it was in my control. I continued to prove myself and perform, if not outperform, a lot of the green berets.

I will share this part of my story because it is relevant to my transition out of the military. In 2015, I was a key leader in running an assessment and selection process. We were on day one of this assessment and selection, which took place on the ranges of Fort Carson, Colorado. There are many dirt roads on the south side, and my mentor, myself, and a medic had to cut across these dirt roads to place cones for an event. We approached a civilian vehicle from the rear, and a man was kneeling in front of the vehicle as we were driving by. We thought that it was very strange but continued on the mission. We drove back 45 minutes later, and he had taken his life with a gunshot wound to the head. We had to stand by him until the authorities could get there. It is a vision that

I will never forget for many reasons, but one was that it was my first exposure to suicide in any capacity.

The rest of my active-duty career was full of ups and downs. I got a divorce and battled with alcohol, which got in the way at times. I met my second wife and thought I had finally found the person I'd be with forever. She was incredibly supportive of everything, and after a deployment and receiving my Bachelor's Degree in Criminal Justice with a Focus on Forensics, I thought it was time for me to transition out of the military to go after a civilian job in law enforcement while joining the National Guard. I completed transitioning courses in late 2019, right before 2020. All the way up to August of 2020, when I was officially off of active duty, I really did not have to show up to work. My plan for exiting was to run my own personal training business while getting my master's degree.

There were many briefs before exiting active duty, which I think is great. And then, there was someone assigned to your exit process who made sure your plan was in place for the day you stepped out into the civilian world. There were job fairs on post, a program to become a teacher, and guidance for going to college. All of these things were nice, but the transition to the Veteran's Affairs process was lacking. Again, there were briefs on how these organizations could help us, but it was one of those experiences where it was "We briefed you so you know everything now, and we can check this block." But let's be honest, no one is going to remember every little thing that is briefed, which I'll get to more later as well.

There I was, off into the civilian world. I became a corrections officer in the Colorado National Guard while doing government contracting, running my own traveling personal training business, and getting my master's degree. It was six months after I left active duty that I would find out one of my buddies in the military, a green beret, would take his life while I was working with my old unit. It was one of those where you just did not see it coming.

I certainly had to work through the thoughts of wondering if there was anything that I could have done. But you can't think that way because it will eat you from the inside out. It sat with me, though. This was the closest I had been to suicide at this time, and I just could not understand it.

I used to be a soldier who never turned down an opportunity. If a school was offered training was offered, I took it. I did what I had to do to get promoted and took on extra responsibilities when I could. My life changed when my wife died by suicide. The person that I used to be was no longer. I had completed my master's degree a month before my wife died, and I thought that the military and law enforcement would forever be a part of me. But all of that disappeared in a moment. I no longer knew who I was.

I was diagnosed with PTSD, anxiety, and depression. I will say that I was at my unit in Denver on the last day of annual training when my wife drove to a trailhead and took her life with my gun. And my National Guard unit was there for me. They were incredibly supportive and allowed me to take care of whatever I needed. One part of the process that was upsetting was dealing with the Army and life insurance. I believe that the individual in charge of helping me with the paperwork was not professional because of my same-sex marriage. They were unresponsive and went as far as to blame me for the paperwork being delayed, even though it was done under his guidance. This was truly the first time that I felt this way, and it was during the worst time of my life.

I tried continuing in the National Guard, even obtaining a promotable status as a Staff Sergeant and potentially the role of a Platoon Sergeant. But I started having panic attacks at the thought of handling a firearm again, and that is when I had to make the decision that if I could not perform a basic soldier task of handling a firearm, then I should not be in the Army anymore. My world became smaller, and I did not function like I used to. It was scary. I decided it was time that I go through the channels to get medically discharged from the Army. Being an Army soldier was something I loved so much; it was a huge part of who I was, but I had to let that soldier go.

Going through the medical board was a waiting game. You fill out a document, and then you wait to hear back about the next step. The process is not difficult, going through the exams, and keeping in touch with your contact as necessary. But I was again faced with many briefs and phone conversations as the transitioning process took place. Lots of information was thrown at me, including emails, documents with charts, and tons of information, and my brain could not keep up with the amount of information I was given. I stand with the fact that information is given to veterans as a check the block. But my brain does not work that way anymore. I found myself getting off long phone calls and totally forgetting what the conversation was even about. I tried to take notes, but a lot of the information that was given ran together. It was all new information and a lot of it. As soon as I received my retirement orders, those individuals assigned to me and my case were no longer there, and I never heard from them again.

One of the things I was surprised about regarding the medical board process was that there were not many conversations about lifestyle after the Army. When it comes to the medical portion, the resources are there; they take care of you. But if you go through the medical board process, make sure you have a plan for a job and what you are going to be doing afterward.

Transitioning to become a civilian was not a difficult process for me when it came to paperwork. I have always been one to make sure paperwork was turned in right away to not create a delay or waste anyone's time. The most difficult part of transitioning for me is having to come to terms with no longer being a soldier. I was a soldier for thirteen years, and I fell in love with it quickly. I love the military and every opportunity I was given, every school I went to (more than most green berets), and the friendships I made through those years. There is nothing like being a soldier, in my opinion. That was my purpose for my old normal. My new normal is full of a different purpose of raising awareness of suicide prevention and mental health. Though I'm not in the Army anymore, that soldier in me continues to drive towards being successful and making achievements. That fire in me still exists. I'm just using it as a tool in a civilian capacity to change lives and inspire others. Even though I miss the Army soldier, I embrace the strength I developed and continue to use daily.

ALICIA NOLAN

ARMY

STAFF SERGEANT

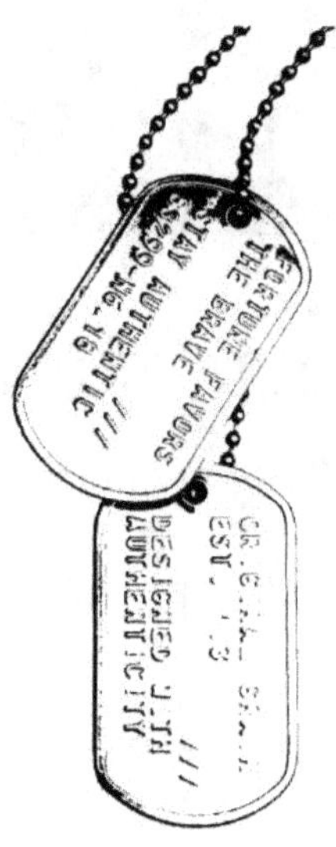

THE STORY OF VETERAN

MALIK LESTAGE

BREAKING BOUNDARIES: A PATH TO REDEMPTION AND RESILIENCE

Introduction: A Glimpse into Childhood and Early Influences

Growing up as the middle child in a family of five in Southern Florida was a blend of structure and subtle rebellion. My parents, steadfast in their commitment to instill discipline and the importance of education, cultivated a home environment that many would consider ideal. Martial arts classes were a staple meant to teach self-discipline and focus. Yet, beneath the surface of this structured upbringing, I felt the constraints of societal norms and the limitations they unknowingly imposed on our minds.

The neighborhood was a tapestry of influences— some uplifting, others misleading. While my parents worked tirelessly to keep us on the right path, the allure of the unknown beckoned me. Early exposure to adult themes like pornography and sex stemmed from a mix of self-discovery and the whispers of a world beyond our front door. These experiences, though confusing, ignited a curiosity about life that went beyond the confines of our community.

The Allure and Disillusionment of Military Life

Joining the military was an impulsive decision, a leap into the unknown that I believed would offer structure and purpose beyond the traditional route of college and a nine-to-five job. The idea of serving something greater than myself was intoxicating. Enlisting out of Southern Florida was a highlight—a chance to build a legacy and surround myself with individuals from diverse backgrounds, all united by a common goal.

Initially, the military fulfilled its promise. The camaraderie, the sense of belonging, and the exposure to different cultures were invigorating. I was part of a brotherhood, training, eating, and facing challenges together. However, the rigidity of military life soon began to chafe. The same structure I had sought started to feel suffocating. Clashes with authority became frequent, whether it was heated exchanges during morning formations or bending the rules to seek moments of freedom off-base.

One incident stands out vividly. Defying orders, I reclaimed my confiscated car to go on a date, only to oversleep and miss a mandatory formation the next morning. The repercussions were severe—an explosive confrontation that escalated my stress and led to a moment of emotional crisis. Reacting impulsively, I sent out a mass text threatening harm to myself and others—a cry for help that I barely understood myself.

The Descent: Struggles with Mental Health, Addiction, and Homelessness

The aftermath was a whirlwind of psychological evaluations and a stint in military correctional custody that lasted longer than basic training. It was a period marked by fear, anger, and a profound sense of isolation. I grappled with feelings of unworthiness and the realization that wearing the uniform did not shield anyone from personal demons.

Upon discharge, life didn't get easier. Stripped of the structure I had both loved and loathed, I found myself homeless on the streets of San Diego. Addiction became a coping mechanism—a way to numb the pain and silence the thoughts of failure that echoed in my mind. Yet, even in the darkest moments, a spark of resilience remained.

Discovering David Goggins' 4x4x48 challenge in 2020 was a turning point. Running had always been a release for me, and this challenge pushed me physically and mentally beyond my limits. It was more than just a physical feat; it was a battle against my inner demons. Each mile was a step towards reclaiming control over my life.

Unexpected Connections and the Importance of Mentorship

During this tumultuous time, unexpected connections provided glimmers of hope. While canvassing for a political campaign, I met a fellow veteran who was also navigating homelessness. Our shared experiences forged a quick bond, and in an act of mutual support, we decided to embark on a spontaneous trip to Las Vegas. It was a brief escape from reality, filled with late-night runs and deep conversations about our pasts and futures.

Mentorship came in the form of individuals who saw beyond my circumstances. One such mentor, empathetic and steadfast, Olajawon Wilson, offered guidance without judgment. He became an anchor, providing financial wisdom when I had none and offering words of wisdom that resonated deeply. His belief in my potential reignited a sense of purpose.

Then, there was Anai Romero, a beacon of light during my darkest days. Her unwavering support and understanding helped me confront my addiction and destructive habits. Through her influence, I began to focus on self-improvement, delving into practices like meditation, journaling, and mindfulness. She taught me the value of emotional intelligence and the importance of nurturing one's soul.

Rebuilding Life and Renewed Purpose

Determined to rebuild, I set out to create a disciplined routine. Physical fitness became a cornerstone—running, calisthenics, and embracing challenges that tested my endurance. I pursued licenses in health and life insurance across California, Florida, and Georgia, venturing into the business world with cautious optimism.

Failures were inevitable, and setbacks were frequent. Entrepreneurial endeavors didn't always pan out, and finding consistent income was a struggle. Family and close relationships sometimes offered more doubt than support. Yet, each obstacle reinforced my determination to keep pushing forward.

I began attending various spiritual gatherings— Seventh-day Adventist services, meetings with Jehovah's Witnesses, and even Sex Addicts Anonymous groups. These experiences broadened my perspective, allowing me to connect with others seeking meaning and healing. Faith became a guiding force, evolving from mere hope into a steadfast belief in a higher purpose.

The Quest for Meaning: Spiritual and Community Engagement

Engaging with the community became a source of fulfillment. I found joy in networking, attending money conferences, and small speaking engagements. Sharing my story was both cathartic and inspiring to others. I realized that my journey, with all its peaks and valleys, could serve as a testament to the power of resilience.

I envisioned organizing events that promoted health and wellness—5K and 10K runs across California beaches, community gatherings that transcended cultural barriers, and initiatives focused on youth engagement and storytelling. The goal was simple: to bring people together, foster understanding, and encourage self-improvement.

Through social media and personal interactions, I offered advice on relationships and personal growth. I became someone others could turn to for encouragement and guidance, leveraging my own experiences to help others navigate their challenges. Even though the most favorable road out of the service was not taken bringing service to the community is a principle that I carry throughout my daily interactions. The importance of this standard alone derives from the exposure of a two-parent household and the love support along with the indestructible bond of my brother Malachi Lestage. Fasting and coming from a healthy household is how my current household will operate especially with the admiration and affirmation from my beautiful wife and daughter.

Conclusion: A Message of Hope and Determination

Looking back, my journey has been anything but linear. It's a tapestry woven with threads of hardship, discovery, failure, and triumph. I've learned that every setback is an opportunity for growth and every challenge a chance to redefine oneself.

The path to redemption is not easy, nor is it quick. It requires confronting one's deepest fears, embracing vulnerability, and persevering despite the odds. But it's a path worth taking. Through discipline, faith, and the support of those who believe in us, we can break boundaries—both those imposed upon us and those we place on ourselves.

My story is not just about personal redemption; it's a testament to the resilience that exists within all of us. I hope that by sharing my journey, others will find the strength to face their own challenges, to seek help when needed, and to never lose sight of the potential that lies within.

Epilogue

As I continue on this path, I remain committed to personal growth and to making a positive impact. Whether through community engagement, mentorship, or simply being a listening ear, I strive to be a catalyst for change. The journey is ongoing, and while the destination remains uncertain, the lessons learned along the way are invaluable.

Ultimately, it's about more than just overcoming adversity—it's about transforming it into a source of strength and inspiration. It's about understanding that our stories, no matter how tumultuous, have the power to uplift others. And it's about recognizing that redemption is not a destination but a continuous journey toward becoming the best version of ourselves.

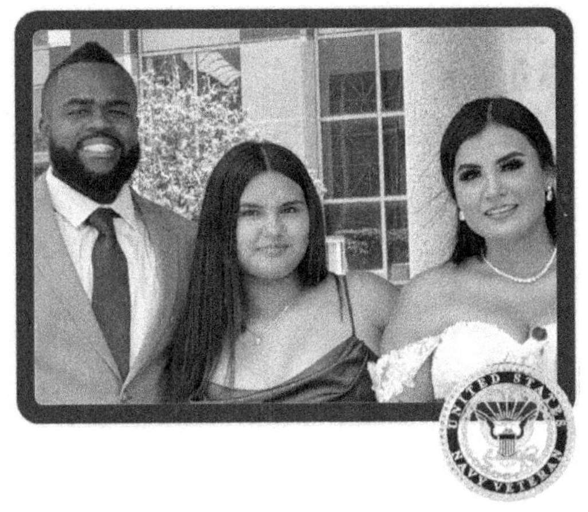

MALIK LESTAGE

NAVY

E-3

THE STORY OF VETERAN

MARC ROJAS

Without a doubt in my mind, my plan was to be a career soldier in the United States Army. I mean, why not? It was a very stable job, provided all the benefits my family would need, most of our living expenses were covered while residing on post, and a far better upbringing for my six kids, rather than being on the brink of them living back in Detroit. Most importantly, the benefits of being in the Army brought me peace of mind. In fact, more peace of mind than I could have ever realized.

Well, this is life, and sometimes life suddenly and abruptly has other plans in store.

I was seven years in, and I had just missed earning E-6 by my own doing. I had the promotion points; however, it was after the first month that the Army's online promotion points system changed. We had to submit promotion points for ourselves, as opposed to our admin clerks doing it for us. I submitted them accurately, but I missed initialing the last page on the website, so the points weren't finalized. I was devastated.

I wouldn't say I was the hardest-charging soldier, but through my best efforts, the command gave me a fair amount of respect. I acted in the place of my platoon sergeant when he was gone, attended the platoon sergeant meetings, reported to brigade monthly reports (BMR) meetings, and was often assigned tasks above my rank, like Brigade Master Driver's Trainer. My annual performance evaluation was nearly immaculate, leaving little room to improve and the comments section read, "Recommend promoting ahead of peers." So, without hesitation, my command sent me to Basic Noncommissioned Officer Course (BNOC) a.k.a. Staff Sergeant School. It was the first step, and I felt honored that my command treated me like a priority and valued me as a leader. Little did I know that first step was going to lead to a career-ending fall.

Before I get into what happened at BNOC and what led to an early, unexpected, unprepared, life-changing exit out of military service, I need to take a few steps back and tell you where I initially came from.

Around 1995, I was diagnosed with bipolar and was in and out of hospital stays for roughly two years. The length of my hospital stays varied. Finding a medicinal cocktail that would balance me out varied as well. Some stays lasted under two weeks, while others lasted up to two months. I would have hyper-manic episodes that would have me feeling euphoric, followed by huge disastrous crashes. It's a story we've all heard before, so I won't get into details. Sometime around 1997, something clicked. I was suddenly better, and I was better without medication. I always had a history of tapering myself off medications. My ego was always in disbelief that I had bipolar disorder. I have always felt it was just the way I was handling life's ups and downs, everyone has ups and downs, everyone has their extremes, and everyone handles life differently. From 1997 to the present day, I've never, ever, ever used bipolar as an excuse for my actions, feelings, or failures, and I've never felt sorry for myself. From that point on, I went on to have a few minor successes. I graduated near the top of my class in broadcasting school and even gave a speech at graduation. I spent a few exciting years in Radio and even won a Michigan broadcasting award. In 2001, with a pre-existing bipolar condition, I enlisted in the military. A decade had passed from ever making an excuse, but in 2007, I believe it was the stigma of bipolar disorder that ended up excusing me. After what happened to me at BNOC, the Army and my command decided to excuse me as well.

I've always felt like I was in really good touch with myself. I was able to find my own balance. I could feel the signs of possibly becoming manic or maybe feeling a little too high on life, so mentally, I had ways of grounding myself. I also knew when I was headed on a downward spiral, and mentally, I could talk myself out of that rut. I never told myself it was bipolar disorder. It was just the way I was handling life for the moment, and it would pass. I grew a habit of telling myself that "everything works out in the end," and it would always manifest everything working itself out.

Sometime around 2004-05, after a successful deployment in Iraq, after getting promoted to sergeant, after earning promotable status, after nearly maxing physical training tests continuously, after graduating from Warrior Leaders Course, after becoming that soldier that earned his place as acting Platoon Sergeant, after earning the trust of my command, and earning my extra duties as Remedial Physical Fitness Instructor, and Brigade Master Driver's Trainer, and being invited to all the big meetings and being recommended as the soldier who should be promoted before his peers, I finally hit a rut. I felt one of those downward spirals coming from nowhere. I knew the feeling enough to tell myself that maybe it was time to check in with someone. I began always feeling nervous, in a hazy, dreamlike state, losing sleep, being quiet, and always wrapped up in my own head. So, I reached out to mental health and made an appointment to talk with a psychologist.

Don't get me wrong, I was still convinced that I was just dealing with a moment in my life and things would work out in the end. I just needed another person's perspective, a professional one. Fortunately, I met Dr. Hippol, a psychologist. After meeting with Dr. Hippol a few times, he was impressed with hearing about my initial diagnosis and my breakthroughs, and he was the first (and not the last) to tell me that I was clearly in touch with myself. When talking to a professional, I think being completely honest with yourself is most important. Without that complete honesty, no one can really understand where you may need help. After seeing me for about a month and a half, Dr. Hippol suggested possibly talking to a great psychiatrist about medications to help me get some sleep and possibly balance me out. By that time, I grew a sense of trust in Dr. Hippol because his feedback was in-depth, and he was engaged with everything I had to talk about. So, I agreed to see his recommended psychiatrist, Captain Petrovic.

Dr. Hippol and Capt. Petrovic worked side by side with me. Petrovic eventually found a good concoction of medications for me. I had a sleep aid, a daily med, a med for side effects, and a med for anxious moments. From then on, I was straight as an arrow, and life was back to normal. Both agreed that any other soldier would have been medically discharged for being prescribed that mix of medications. Because of everything I shared with Dr. Hippol and the breakthrough I had experienced, my achievements, and my forward progress, despite my diagnosis, they allowed me to fly under the radar and continue with my promising career. I was appreciative and did just that. I continued forward.

Around September of 2007, my command put me on orders to go to Maryland for BNOC, and it was exciting. School was going to be about three months long, so I had to get all my prescriptions in advance. Then, a series of unfortunate events happened. My first plane en-route to Maryland had a huge delay, causing me to miss a connecting flight. The airport had to give me a hotel voucher to stay overnight. It was a very late night, to an early wake-up. I don't believe I slept a wink for fear of missing another flight. That delay caused a hiccup in my car rental situation when I finally got to Maryland, plus I had about an hour's drive ahead of me. I finally made it to Aberdeen Proving Grounds after 0400 on the first day of BNOC. Staff duty at the welcome center informed me that first formation was at 0600, as they assigned my quarters.

I barely had a wink of sleep during my trip due to the stress and anxiety that seeded from the initial flight delay. Dealing with my rental car situation only added to the strain. Getting to BNOC as late as I did, with little time to recover, aggravated my situation even more.

Staff duty handed me a standard operating procedures (SOP) pamphlet for my quarters. The SOP was a detailed list of how my room was supposed to be displayed down to the exact measurements, and this was to be completed by the end of the day and subject to inspection. I was already behind the power curve since most of the soldiers arrived over the weekend and had ample time to have their rooms "dress right dress" to standard. I figured I'd go to my room and get that started since I wasn't getting to bed anyhow. Wrong. When I got to my quarters, I discovered I had a roommate there, tucked in and sleeping. Needless to say, this magnified everything I was feeling.

After roll call formation at 0600, my platoon marched over to a nearby classroom for a briefing with our platoon sergeant and to introduce ourselves to one another. There were only about 10 of us, including myself. During that initial briefing, our Platoon Sergeant wanted a Platoon Guide appointed and asked for a volunteer. After a moment of uncomfortable silence that felt like it lasted forever, me being me in this situation enthusiastically raised my hand and said, "I'll do it." The Platoon Sergeant acknowledged and told me to meet him back in the classroom by 0800. We were released for breakfast chow, and the next formation would be at 0900. I already knew this was a bad decision, and I was nowhere near prepared for the tasks that lied ahead.

I had no appetite, so I skipped eating chow. I was in my head and knew I had to do something about it. I had to reach for my medication that was prescribed for anxious moments such as this. It was a Xanex. I rarely used it, and Capt. Petrovic only scripted me 6 per month, with the direction to only use half a pill "as needed." Mind you, I had 3 months' worth due to my advanced allotment, plus some. From that first half of a pill to the end of the day, things became very hazy.

At 0800, I met with the Platoon Sergeant. He gave me a laundry list of tasks to complete by the next day, which included mostly initial admin work, collecting platoon personnel's information for accountability, making duty rosters, and assigning others' responsibilities. By 0900, we were in formation and marching to our first day of class orientation. With each class, we veteran given a syllabus with more tasks and deadlines for things to be completed by tomorrow. We were eventually released for Lunch. I remember still not having much of an appetite, but I did force-feed something down for my own good. Feeling overwhelmed with how everything began, desperate to calm my nerves, I found some time to run over to my quarters and grab another half pill. From there on, I only recall very few parts of the day.

I don't recall how the rest of the day of school went, but I do remember when we got back to the barracks, we learned that it was our platoon's night to clean our floors and the stairwells. Luckily, my platoon took the initiative and started taking on that task without direction. I went to my room and started to get everything to SOP with the help of my roommate as I simultaneously worked on the tasks that were due tomorrow for both my Platoon Sergeant and school. Unfortunately, things didn't end there, and I'm pretty sure I completely missed dinner. By this time, I had taken another half pill or two. People from my platoon were consistently knocking on my door with questions, and then I was informed of an impromptu Platoon Leaders' meeting scheduled for 1900 in the first-floor common area. That was the last I remember of just about anything.

I don't believe I ever made it to the Platoon Leaders' meeting. I only remember glimpses of that night. I remember reaching for the bottle of Xanex multiple times, I remember seeing my Platoon Sergeant, I remember an ambulance trip to the ER, and I remember requesting a cherry-flavored charcoal to drink, and I recall having a tube shoved down my nose. After that, I remember coming back to total consciousness a few days later at Walter Reed Hospital, sitting in front of a television watching The People's Court. About two weeks later, I was on a flight back to Fort Wainwright. It wasn't the homecoming I was expecting.

The first day I reported back to my unit, the sounds around my presence were crickets. From then on, I barely heard a word from my command. Those who were closest to me didn't inquire about what happened, and most of the lower enlisted just thought I was away on an extended leave. It was like absolutely nothing happened. I saw Capt. Petrovic and Dr. Hippol a few times following my return. Unfortunately, Capt. Petrovic was taken out of the picture due to reassignment. So, I was assigned to a new psychiatrist, Major Vince. After my initial visit with Maj. Vince, I was immediately under the impression that she already had her mind set to recommend medical discharge. How could I blame her? She didn't know me as well as Capt. Petrovic, and I was just a stranger. I don't think she was comfortable with prescribing my medications. I couldn't expect her to bless off on continuing to keep me flying under the radar, no matter how good of a soldier I was, no matter how much I had progressed.

After a few weeks of hearing nothing from my command, I was finally summoned to my commander's office. I was briefly asked about my experience at BNOC. As I explained the events that took place, I felt like my commander was just going through the motions of pretending to listen. As soon as I was done, he had no questions or any type of feedback. At that moment, he informed me that I would be assigned to the Warrior's Transition Unit (WTU) and I'd begin out processing from the military by medical discharge, through the recommendation of Maj. Vince. I wouldn't hear anything more from the upper echelon in my company again. I didn't feel I was owed any kind of recognition from my command, but I was the longest-standing soldier in my command. After spending over six years in my company and elevating from standing last in my ranks to being the soldier standing in front of my platoon's formations, I found it sad that my departure was reduced to a whisper in the wind. One day, I just wasn't there anymore. It felt like everything I worked for was all in vain. My soldiers in my platoon presented me with a plaque and desk clock that were both etched "The Original Old Duke," which I was beyond appreciative of, and it helped cushion the overall blow.

While at WTU, I continuously appealed my discharge with no luck. I was told I had three attempts to appeal. Eventually, I was told I used all my appeals. It really didn't feel like any of my pleads went anywhere. I just kept being told no. I wasn't given forms to fill out, and I wasn't given a board of people to talk to or assigned to anyone to address my case. I was just told my appeal was denied. I was still trying to be a soldier. I even requested and was allowed to participate and sing cadence for my former company when they had their next battalion run. My first line sergeant and platoon sergeant at WTU both made some noble attempts to advocate for me to stay in, but it fell on deaf ears. I was just pushed along through the Army Career and Alumni Program (ACAP) process.

I do consider myself fortunate. Prior to the BNOC fiasco, I had built a good rapport with a government contractor. Their mobile maintenance section worked out of a mobile trailer office in the parking lot of our motor pool. There wasn't much to offer, just a very small office in our shop for them to operate out of. It didn't fit everyone, but it was a lot warmer than their current situation. Just before leaving for WTU, their supervisor learned of my situation, and he offered me a position as lead inspector and equipment operator's trainer. There was one stipulation: I needed a Commercial Driver's License (CDL) to qualify for the position. I was on the fence about the possibility of staying in Alaska or going back to Michigan. The offer couldn't have come at a better time because I had no idea what I was going to do for work.

I truly thought that ACAP would help point me in the right direction to getting my CDL, considering I already had a job lined up. I couldn't have been more wrong. ACAP felt like running on a treadmill. I was checking the boxes and getting the required initials. Was I really getting anywhere, was I getting any help? I was filling out a bunch of paperwork, making a bunch of out-processing appointments, reworking my resume several times, and listening to seminars. My questions were vaguely answered, and the only people ACAP seemed to focus on were the full-term retirees. I'm still not sure that I completely out-processed ACAP. I would eventually be given my "Honorable Discharge" papers, a small severance, and a five percent disability rating, and I was no longer in the Army. After that, I had no real direction.

No one had really prepared me for what was to come. ACAP didn't explain the culture shock I was going to experience in the civilian world. No one explained the actual costs of living, renting a house, utilities, medical, dental, and vision insurance, and no longer having access to the commissary and post exchange for groceries and goods. I didn't know I'd be hemorrhaging so much money. I didn't know I'd go through a period of working up to four jobs seven days a week for over two years while my wife worked as well and raised six children. Over time and years of hard work and promotions, everything eventually improved.

ACAP was just putting me through a process of checking boxes, getting initials, and being given vague seminars. I desperately knocked on doors, looking for answers from anyone who would listen. I felt I had exhausted every option until one day, an older gentleman overheard my story from another room and invited me into his office. He made a call to Mr. Sheehan, someone he knew at the Fairbanks Department of Labor (DOL). I finally had an appointment with someone who may be able to help me.

Though it was a unique situation for the DOL to get involved, Mr. Sheehan said that he would try and help. The DOL was in the business of offering services to people who didn't have jobs. Technically, I was still employed and collecting a paycheck with the US ARMY, so it was harder to justify assisting me. I don't know how Mr. Sheehan made it happen, but he found a way to have my CDL training and certification paid for, along with rent for our first house and other expenses through our transition. I had expected ACAP to offer this kind of assistance, but they didn't. It was that gentleman who happened to overhear my story and Mr. Sheehan at the DOL who made my transition successful. I was out of the military on a Friday and started government contracting that following Monday. Within six years, I had been promoted to Maintenance Supervisor, Operations Manager & Assistant Program Manager. Since then, I had a few other successful jobs, went back to military contracting, and eventually became a full-time government employee.

ACAP has changed to the Soldier For Life Transition Assistance Program (SFL-TAP), which offers more services.

The military now offers the Career Skills Program (CSP), where soldiers can work as civilian interns, which leads to jobs prior to transitioning out of the military. Regardless of what is available, never stop asking questions and beating on doors, expect the unexpected, build relationships, always have a savings to fall back on, and have a career after the military in mind. Always know that everything will work itself out in the end.

MARC ROJAS

ARMY

OCTOBER 2000- SEPTEMBER 2008

SGT, E-5

THE STORY OF VETERAN

DAVID KELLEY

Born in Waco Texas, I spent my formative years in Odessa, Texas and Rising Star, Texas where athletics was a large part of growing up. My high school years were in Belton Texas where I was fortunate enough to have played football, baseball, and track. Graduated high school in 1977. From high school, I was awarded a football scholarship to Cisco Junior College. After completing my freshman year, I did not return to Cisco. One year of college behind me but no real plan and or idea as to what to do with my life. I found myself drifting in life with no real purpose or direction. In April of 1979, I walked into the Navy Recruit

Center in Temple Texas and told the lead recruiter that I wanted to join the Navy. Having not done any research into the Navy opportunities or requirements, I presented my ASVAB scores. Based upon those scores the recruiter showed me what opportunities / rates, were available to me. April 27, 1979, at age 19 I enlisted in the United States Navy as a Boiler Technician. I am going to be a BT.

As the saying goes, choose your rate, choose your fate. Truer words of wisdom that would resonate with me throughout my navy career and beyond. After eight weeks of boot camp in San Diego, and upon graduation our company had six hours liberty. Next morning eighteen "new boots" from San Diego Recruit Training Center, Company 087 were headed to A school and flew out to Navy Training Center, Great Lakes, Illinois. Also known as Great Mistakes.

Before departing from San Diego, the daily temperature had hovered around 95 degrees. Short sleeve weather. Arriving in Chicago, at O'Hare airport the temperature was near 55 degrees. A 40-degree temperature drop. All eighteen of us, "new boots" were dressed in our summer uniform. A thin cotton short-sleeve shirt and pants. Exiting from the plane, we quickly headed to pick up our luggage. While waiting on our sea bags, there was a collective shivering and teeth chattering. Ripping open our sea bags each new boot retrieved anything long sleeve. Lesson learned, when traveling always hand carry a light jacket and check the weather at your destination.

Fast forward to A School, which was completed in about 3 months. The A school itself was a self-paced introduction to the fundamentals of mechanics and boiler operations. Immediately after completing A school, I flew home for two-weeks of leave and a two-week assignment in the Navy's recruiter assistant program. This put me back home for a month. Then on to my first ship the USS Barry DD-933 that was home ported in Mayport, Florida. Two boiler rooms, two engine rooms. Four D-type boilers, 1200psi steam at 1000+ degrees. And all the auxiliary equipment. Feed pumps that took sea water and forced it into the boilers. Reducers, valves, fuel pumps, fire, heat and no ac just outside air forced into the boiler room space.

At times, the ambient temperature in the space was 110-115 degrees. Between the two main feed pumps it would reach 150-160 degrees and higher. Work schedule while underway was at times exhausting. Depending on your shift, a sailor could be working 16 hours a day. If you had the 4-8 watch that meant you were on duty manning the boilers from 4am to 8am, then a regular workday 8am to 4pm, then back on duty for the evening shift of 4pm to 8pm. While on active duty dand being a snipe on board a steam driven ship meant that you were sweaty, dirty, oily, and stinky. Oh, the glamourous life of a sailor! Fast forward a few years and while in college, I was informed by one of my professors that being in the Navy is the closest thing to indentured servitude. That statement stuck with me.

My Expectations

At the end of my 3-year contract, I was ready to get out of active duty. Upon departing from the ship, I was paid for my unused leave days and had a pocketful of cash. I had sixty to ninety days before I had to report to a reserve center to begin my Navy Reserve obligations. Within a month I found myself back in Texas and temporarily living with my parents. Within a few weeks I found a job working at a hospital in the maintenance department. This hospital had two low-pressure boilers that I was responsible for. The skills learned while on active duty as a boiler technician translated into a maintenance job. The maintenance pay was low, but I had a job and by now I had a place of my own. While on active duty I did participate in the Veterans Education Assistance Program (VEAP). The VEAP was the only educational benefit I was eligible for during the time of my active-duty enlistment. I believe this was a one-to-one contribution. For every dollar I contributed, the government would match. At this point I was ready to resume my college career and enrolled in a few classes at the local junior college.

The Navy Reserves provided me the opportunity to keep one foot in the military and one foot in the civilian world. The Reserve pay was extremely helpful. Plus, I got to go on active-duty orders for 2 weeks once a year. I found that I was always looking forward to traveling. In the words of Winston Churchill "a reservist is twice the citizen". What I was not prepared for in the reserves, is that advancement opportunities seemed to be less or even non-existent compared to active duty. Here is my comparison; during my three years active duty I rose in rank from E1 to E5. The next five years in reserves, getting promoted to E6 was not attainable. Very frustrating. After a combined eight years of active and reserve, it was time to exit the Navy.

For the next few years, I found myself working at dead end jobs. Making enough to survive. Then I had a snow skiing accident which eventually led to surgery on my knee. Finding myself out of a job, no medical insurance, no formal education, I was hit with the realization that I needed to position myself with better opportunities and a game plan for my future. I was in bad shape. That was a wakeup call. Fortunately for me, my parents offered me a place to stay while I got back on my feet. After ten years of being out on my own I found myself dependent on my parents. This was a real blow to my ego, but I sucked it up and enrolled in a 4-year university in my hometown. I had accumulated quite a few college hours over the last ten years; however, the university would only accept two years' worth of college work. A degree plan was set with full time class hours. This afforded me part time work for pocket change. In the fall of 1989, I graduated from the University of Mary-Hardin Baylor with a bachelor's degree in business administration.

Twelve years after graduating from high school I finally earned my undergraduate degree. Persistence and family support were critical elements in achieving this goal. While attending various college's part time over a ten-year period, I had mostly paid out of pocket for tuition. I had not used much of the VEAP monies earned previously. Attending UMHB, a private university, those monies were gone quickly.

If you enlist in the armed forces in Texas, the service member is eligible for the Hazelwood Act. The Hazlewood Act is a State of Texas benefit that provides qualified Veterans, spouses, and dependent children with an education benefit of up to 150 hours of tuition exemption, including most fee charges, at public institutions of higher education in Texas. This does not include living expenses, books, or supply fees. I could not take advantage of the Hazelwood educational opportunities for my undergraduate degree because of attending a private university.

Time to find a "real" job. Looking around for that career path I went into public education. My first teaching gig was with my high school alma mater. I taught special education and coached girls' soccer. What an unforgettable experience.

In 1994, I re-enlisted in the Navy Reserves. Having accumulated 8 years of service I did not want to throw away that service time. But this time I was not going in as a boiler technician. I re-enlisted as an Information Technician. Computers had always interested me, and the opportunity presented itself.

As a classroom teacher I was not making much money. Seeing the need to further my education, I moved to San Antonio, Texas. There are a lot of state schools in San Antonio and the Hazelwood Act would be greatly beneficial. After a few years of teaching, I applied to a master's program in Educational Leadership at the University of Texas at San Antonio. In May 1999, I received my Master of Arts in Educational Leadership. The Hazelwood Act paid for about 95% of this program. Opportunities began to open in the educational arena. This propelled me to my first assistant principal position at an Alternative Educational Program.

During my first year as assistant principal at AEP, I applied to and was accepted into the UTSA Educational Doctorate program. The program commenced in the fall of 2001. I had over one hundred hours left to use in the Hazelwood Act. This benefit was going to pay for the doctorate program. Classes began in August 2001. We met as a cohort Tuesday, Thursday and every other Saturday. Then 9/11 happened. I was mobilized to active-duty November 2001. The horrendous events of 9/11 changed the world forever.

November of 2001 I was mobilized and back on active duty. I had a wife, four children ages 9 - 1, and a home mortgage. I was really leaning into the Lord during this time. Initial recall orders indicated a one-year mobilization, but my orders were reduced to eight months. Being mobilized in the middle of the fall semester left a large hole to fill for the AEP campuses. When I returned to civilian life mid-June, my assistant principal position at the AEP had been filled. Due to the Uniformed Services Employment and Reemployment Act of 1994 the school district had to offer me a similar or in-kind position. An assistant principal position was offered at a middle school.

The transition process from active duty to reserve status was more of a mental challenge than anything else. My experience as a reserve member being mobilized emphasized the importance of taking care of home and job responsibilities. Emotions can become a hurdle. They get strained and become very raw and at this point, I must emphasize the importance of having a relationship with the Lord.

After three years as an assistant principal at Rudder Middle School Northside ISD, I was mobilized once again to active duty. Mobilization orders were for a year. So, I planned for and prepared the family for the upcoming year. This mobilization would put me out of touch with the family for a few weeks to a month at a time. This was important for the family to understand. About eight months into this mobilization, we received word to stand down. We were being demobilized. The transition process from active duty to civilian began. At this point in my Navy career, I had just over seventeen years of service. The opportunity to stay on active-duty orders at a joint base presented itself.

For the next three and half years I was on active-duty orders. During this time, I was selected and promoted to Navy Chief. For enlisted Navy personnel being selected and promoted to Chief was a huge career accomplishment. My responsibilities and job opportunities increased exponentially. I was up to my neck in information technology duties. Training and certifications were abundant and seemed never ending. Senior leadership drilled into my head that the Navy should offer every opportunity to prepare its members for life outside the Navy. Focusing on the technology, I tried to take advantage of every training or certification opportunity possible.

Having been mobilized twice since 9/11, benefits came in several forms. As a veteran, I had taken advantage of VA

Home loans. Over the years I was able to use these tools and purchase several homes. VA educational benefits, as stated earlier I took advantage of both federal and state opportunities. The VEAP for my undergraduate degree.

Hazelwood Act and federal VA Educational benefits for both the Master of Education and a master's in Business Administration (MBA).

Little did I know that the accumulated experiences gained on active duty and in the civilian arena would lead me to becoming the Chief of Information Technology for the Joint Electromagnetic Warfare Center at Lackland AFB. A joint military operation that included uniform service members, foreign service members, government members, and contractors.

Lessons learned

Planning is paramount to success; it is one half of the equation. Plan your work, work your plan. Make a one-year plan. A 5-year plan. A 20-year plan. Plans do change. That is ok. Stay flexible. Opportunities will pop up unexpectedly. One never knows when or where opportunities will arise. As that great baseball philosopher Yogi Berra once stated: when you come to a fork in the road take it.

Before entering into any contract, read it in its entirety. The big print giveth. The small print taketh. Do your homework.

Write things down. Once you commit your thoughts to paper, it becomes more concrete. You can read, re-read and plan out your action-plan. There is a psychological benefit of writing things down. It releases the mind of having to constantly remember.

Trust but verify. You must watch your own back. When someone says that they will do something for you, trust them that they will but check on the results. Check that they have followed through and have fulfilled commitment. It seems that the days of a verbal agreement and a handshake are from an era of the past.

Get as much education as you can. This can be formal (college) or informal (trade school, on-line, life) education. One never knows how education can shape your future.

Family support plays a critical role in life

More importantly, make Jesus your Lord and Savior; lean into Him. Establish and grow in that relationship. One never knows when you will be called home to account for your life. Jesus is the best life compass when it comes to making decisions.

DAVID KELLEY

NAVY

CHIEF PETTY OFFICER

THE STORY OF VETERAN

TIMOTHY CARL STAGGS

My name is Timothy Carl Staggs. I was raised in one house in a rural area of Palestine, Arkansas. I was never exposed to the military in my family. The first I ever heard about the military as an option for a career was when I got a call one day from an Air Force recruiter asking if I would like to join. I had been praying for what I was going to do with my life in May 1980 after graduation. I knew that I did not want to stay in a small farming community where I could work as a farm laborer, in a grocery store, or a factory. And I wasn't ready for college.

So, the Air Force recruiter asked if I wanted to join and without thinking really hard about it I said, "Yes."

In September of that year, I was off on a new adventure in the Air Force. I really didn't know if I would like the Air Force and would be willing to stay in for 20 years. After serving for 3 years, I had to make a choice as to whether or not I would sign up for another 4 years. I applied for a different job as an Aircraft Airframe specialist and did get orders to this new job. I had been an Aircraft Armament Systems Specialist and although it was fun loading bombs on aircraft it didn't satisfy my true desire. I had asked for a small wheel mechanic job so I could have a skill when and if I decided to leave the Air Force. I asked for this job, but the recruiter who was placing me in the job the Air Force needed pointed to a picture where these guys were working on an airplane and said, "This will fit you perfectly. An Aircraft Armament System specialist. In other words, I would load bombs on aircraft. We had a saying, "Without us the Air Force would be just another airline." That was true, but it was far from being an auto technician.

My first duty station after basic and technical school was Torrejon, AB Spain. I looked at these orders and said out loud, "TorreJOHN, (my pronunciation) Spain! I don't want to go there! What happened to Barksdale, Louisiana just one state below Arkansas. Or Little Rock, Arkansas just 70 miles from home! I later realized they had no fighter jets at this base. This was another disappointment the Air Force did to me. I later found that this assignment was the best assignment for me. I was new to my Christian faith and was raised in a small Assembly of God church—a Pentecostal church. I had my fears of going to Spain and there wouldn't be a Pentecostal church to attend, but I didn't know that there indeed was a Pentecostal church there.

I arrived in Spain on a Saturday evening. I found where I was supposed to stay for the night. I was tired. I had never flown in a plane for over 6 hours. I went to bed as soon as I got there but on that Sunday morning I searched for a church. I found the Base Chapel and looked on the board outside and it listed a Christian Servicemen's Center, a Pentecostal Fellowship was having a service that night at 6:00 P.M. I just shouted Hallelujah. Thank you, Jesus. I will have a place to have fellowship and worship God.

While serving in that church as a van driver, I began to hear the stories of those in the van. I began to pray for them during my nightly prayers. This was where God began calling me to be a pastor of a church. This happened during the second year of my assignment.

My second assignment was at Fairchild, AFB in Spokane, Washington. This time my choice was honored for I had picked to go to this state. I wanted to see what it was like on the west coast. I moved there in March of 1983 and again I found a church to attend off base. I still remembered the call God had put on my life but just didn't know how it was going to work out. Would I just preach from church to church? Would I serve in a church as an associate pastor? All I knew at the time was I didn't want to be in the Air Force any longer and decided to get out in September of 1984. I served 4 years in the Air Force and looking back it was the best decision I ever made at that point in my life. Our High School graduation class had a motto, "Expanding Your Horizons." I do believe that the Air Force expanded my outlook on life.

I remember the time I was getting close to getting out. I began to wonder how was I going to make it on my own. All this time I had a place to stay. A guaranteed monthly income, which was not a lot, but it did provide all my needs, just not my wants. I remember asking my pastor what I was going to do. Spokane was a large city. I was just a country boy from Arkansas. It helped having someone to talk to and my Lord to pray to. I did come to understand that I would be OK and would find a job. Which I did find one at a Subaru place as a service man who cleaned all the cars coming in for service and other odd jobs around the shop. My hope was to move into a mechanic job. Maybe they would even train me? I thought.

I don't remember one class, briefing or resource that prepared me for this next chapter in my life. I really didn't think it was the Air Force's job to help with this transition. It would have been nice to have had some direction. I did know about the VEAP program. That is, the Vocational Education Assistance Program where all the money you deposited into your education account would be tripled for a college education. At that time in my life, I was not wanting to go to college. Pastors in my denomination did not encourage formal education so I saw no need in it. All I knew was to go from business to business and look for a job. I also looked in the newspaper for jobs. I hated going to a job and being turned down. For some reason, I took it personally and took a lot of courage to ask another place for a job. Again, I was not prepared to face this challenge of finding a new job. I knew God was calling me, but I was not feeling the need or the confidence to go into full time preaching ministry. Nor did I seem to have the confidence to find a new job. This surprises me. I won awards in the Air Force. Like the best Load Crew of the year and the quarter. I even got a chance to fly in an F4 Phantom fighter jet, but they called me on the day before I was to go back to the states for a new duty station.

I did go to this employment office that I discovered in the newspaper. I found this program where I could learn how to be a machinist. During my time in High School, we had a vocational truck to come to our school. There we were exposed to the metal work profession using a press drill, a lathe and other metal cutting and shaping tools. I made a meat tenderizing hammer that I have in our own kitchen. So, this sparked an interest in me, and I found out more information about it. The program required me to go to different shops and tell them about the program that would pay half my wages for a year during the training time. Then I would have a permanent job in their company. Looking back, that was a good opportunity. I just didn't have the courage to go and present this to different employers until I found a place. I landed a job at the Subaru place that only paid half of what I would have made at the machinist apprenticeship.

From this experience, it would have helped me tremendously to have formal training on interviewing and how to show confidence in finding a new job. It would have also helped to know of all the resources and training programs for veterans.

I don't want to end this experience on a bad tone. My time in the Air Force did expand my horizons. It showed me that I was good at working with my hands. It also exposed me to different cultures than my own. I would not do anything differently if given the choice.

I have another transition I went through most recently in 2010. This time in the Army was my most meaningful time of service. Shortly after joining the Air Force on the delayed entry program, I blurted out one day at my Aunt's house that I would be a chaplain in the military one day. At that time, I vaguely knew what this was besides a preacher in the military. I believed that God had put that in my heart and that one day I would be a Chaplain in the military. When I was in basic training in the Air Force, I asked one of our Technical Sergeant's what I had to do to become a Chaplain. He told me to just go away. But a few days later he called me in the office and told me that I needed 4 years of college plus a seminary degree. I was disappointed but also naïve to think all I had to do was ask and I could be a Chaplain. Nevertheless, I still remembered what God had impressed upon me.

A few years after getting out of the Air Force, I got married in 1987. It was then that I sensed God was calling me to go to Lee College, a bible school in Cleveland, Tennessee. We moved from Tacoma, Washington a few months after I was married to Cleveland to start college. At that time, I wasn't 100% sure what I would do with the degree. All I knew was that I wanted to prepare myself more for the ministry. While signing up for classes I went to the financial aid office and while I was there, I saw a brochure for the Army National Guard explaining benefits I could obtain to help me financially while attending school. I called the local National Guard unit which happened to be in Cleveland and within a few weeks I was serving as a reserve weekend Soldier. That next Summer during our annual training in Fort Stewart, Georgia I was reminded once again of God's call for me to be a Chaplain. It was nighttime and I was settling down in my jeep getting ready to get some sleep. I looked up in the sky. It was a beautiful starry night. I again sensed the Lord drawing me to the Military Chaplaincy. This time it was seen as a real possibility because I had the desire to get a degree and was enrolled and completed one year of college. For the next few years, things went pretty smooth at college. I had a tough professor teaching Systematic Theology that was a big challenge. I made an F in the first test I had with him. I was crushed. This was my senior year, and I had never made below a B in all my Bible courses. I was able to pass the class with the lowest score I ever made—a D.

I graduated from college in May of 1991. I enrolled in our denomination's seminary a short distance down the road from the college. I found the first year of Seminary was quite easy. We just had lots of reading and writing but I was able to maintain a good grade point average. At this time, I had an opportunity to get into the Army Chaplain candidate program while I was still in school. Something happened at my local church that caused me to even question whether or not I even wanted to pursue ministry. I was a member of a smaller church where I served in various positions. I was getting the practical experience I needed to qualify as an

Army Chaplain. Our church began to fall apart. Members were slowly leaving to find another church where they "felt" God leading them. There were rumors being spread. Members of our pastors on the deacon board were leaving. I saw this and I personalized it. I questioned the motives of my fellow Christian friends that I had grown to love. I hated seeing the pastor and his wife going through this rejection. I only later learned that I was vicariously experiencing my own rejection of my father. He had left the family when I was only 5 and discovered this in a counseling class at Lee College. I had carried this rejection my whole life after the divorce.

Our pastor did get a vote and was asked to leave. I was there on a Wednesday when I learned of the news. It hit me hard. I ran out the front door of the church and got on my knees and told God, "If this is what ministry is, I don't want any part of it!" This was the start of dark times in our family. I wasn't sure what I was going to do from there. I talked with professors at the school, and they showed me love and care. None of them shamed me for questioning my faith and my call. I tried to continue seminary, but I just couldn't continue. I had no hope. I was so saddened. Then I remembered the first class I had in seminary. This class mentioned several avenues to complete a practicum as one of the requirements of my Master's degree. It was Clinical Pastoral Education (CPE). I would serve in a Hospital as a

Chaplain resident while part of a class and a trained supervisor. I dropped all my courses and immediately enrolled in the CPE program in Chattanooga, Tennessee. I thought this would be a time where I would make sense of what had happened at my local church, but it didn't. I talked about it some but for the most part we discussed my own rejection and victimhood.

I did complete the CPE program and was able to complete the courses I had dropped and continue until graduation in June of 1996. I wasn't sure even then what I was going to do with my degree. I went to our denomination's board to become endorsed to become a Chaplain. They didn't accept me. I was relieved. I knew I wasn't ready. I still had too much hurt that the church split and the pain of what I had learned about myself in CPE to go into the Army as a Chaplain.

In September of 1996 I got a job in our denominational headquarters. I did some writing and phone counseling for our denomination's pastors. It was there that I began to heal of the hurt in the local church. I got involved in a bigger church's counseling department. I attended support groups and was the leader of the ministry for a year.

A few years later the tragic 9/11 event occurred. It was October 31, 2001, that I was training for the Army National Guard. As I was watching the Tanks fire at their targets down the range, I heard in my heart the Lord asking me, "Why ain't you a Chaplain?" I said to myself, "Why ain't I." That was a Sunday and that Monday morning I called the director of our Chaplain's department and told him I wanted to be an Army Reserve chaplain. He agreed and told me the board was meeting on November 7th which happened to be my birthday. I went to the board and was selected. On January 16, 2002, I was selected in the Army National Guard as a Chaplain. God is faithful! In June of 2002 our unit went to Fort Irwin, California for a big training exercise. I went and served as a chaplain and was blown away at the great opportunity I had. I got home from that experience and immediately called our Chaplain's department again where Dr. Robert Crick affirmed my calling, and I was endorsed as an Active-Duty Army Chaplain. My dream had come through.

On January 8th, 2003, I was commissioned as a Chaplain and went to Chaplain's Officer Basic Course in Fort Jackson, South Carolina. I enjoyed my time as a Chaplain. I was stationed as a Basic Training Chaplain in Fort Knox, Kentucky. Working with the trainees and the Soldiers was a challenge for me. The pressures of the everyday schedule got to me, and I began to experience some depression. This made it hard for me to perform my duties. Physical Training was difficult. I failed an annual fitness test which added to my distress. I had thoughts of suicide, and this caused me to seek help from my doctor. He prescribed some medication, and it helped tremendously. My next duty station was at Fort Hood. When I arrived in July of 2005 we were training for our deployment to Iraq. I went on the deployment and performed well. When I got home, I was asked if I wanted to deploy again. I chose not to deploy due to the strain my absence caused on my 6-year-old daughter. I was sent to Fort Knox again. This time I worked with Army Individual Training Soldiers who trained as Bradley mechanics.

Something changed in me after the deployment. I began to lose my interest in the Army. Although I wanted to stay in and retire from Active Duty, I just thought this was my adjustment from the deployment. Nevertheless, I was feeling depressed again. This time I started some counseling and medication for my depression. This depression was again affecting my ministry. I had a hard time having the energy to get out of my office. Each day, I couldn't wait until it was time for me to go home.

In 2009, I was in the promotion zone for the rank of Major. My evaluations had been pretty good, I thought and didn't dream that I would not get selected. I thought God chose me for this so how could I not be selected. In December of that year, I went to the career course for Major. Again, I thought I would get promoted. Why would the Army send me to this course if I wasn't going to get promoted. In the winter of 2010, the results of the board came in and I was not selected! This crushed me emotionally and physiologically. I didn't know what I was going to do to take care of my family. I had this good paying ministry and how was I going to find something else. God strengthened me after this occurred. Through prayer and talking with several people I got my hope back and realized that my career wasn't over. I had one more promotion board to go before I had to get out of the military.

In June of 2010, I got stationed at Fort Campbell, Kentucky in an Air Cavalry unit. I was excited about this unit and looked forward to serving there. We were scheduled to deploy to Afghanistan in the Winter of that year. I did not deploy due to a health reason. Looking back God used this for my good. The board results came out in the Spring of 2011, and I was not selected. To have been in Afghanistan at that time would have been very difficult to prepare for the next chapter of my life.

This time the news was not emotionally taxing on me as it was the first time. I still wasn't sure what I was going to do but I was hopeful that God was going to direct my life. I knew that I would be able to get a job to take care of my family. And that I did. I had a big separation payment, and I had found a CPE residency in Alabama for the next. It was there I worked through my emmotions of being passed over for promotion. I learned my last evaluation was the one that affected my promotion. I felt my Brigade Chaplain did not treat me fairly and it was hard for me to forgive him of this. Healing from this rejection of the Army was like going through a divorce. The Army was still there because I was able to transfer to the Reserves, but it was not the same as being on active duty. Not liking the active component while having to live with the Army as a reservist. I was at least going to obtain a Reserve retirement, so I chose to stay in the Reserves. Nothing could really prepare a Soldier from being passed over from a promotion. The Army did have a week of classes that helped to prepare Soldiers for the civilian workplace, but in my situation nothing they offered helped because I had already found a job. The only transition I needed was to deal with the hurt of the promotion Passover. I felt like I was treated differently by my peers. It seemed they didn't want to associate with someone who was passed over. This transition, though it was emotional, prepared me for my present prison ministry. Also, God has provided every need as if I would have stayed in the military and retired there.

TIMOTHY CARL STAGGS

US AIR FORCE

ARMY NATIONAL GUARD

ACTIVE ARMY CHAPLAIN

ARMY RESERVE CHAPLAIN

THE STORY OF VETERAN

DAVID N. AMMONS, PHD

HAIL TO THE CHIEF (A)

Back in the Day – Why I Joined

This awesome journey really began in High School. I was in the summer between my junior and senior year in high school wondering what I was going to do with my life. I thought I might want to go to college, but I was concerned that it would be difficult to pay for college. I knew my parents would do what they could, but I also knew that as the youngest of six children that the "money spicket" for college was starting to come to a drip, so to speak. My father was a Middle School Teacher, and my mother did not work outside the home. I am thinking it was late June or early July in 1984 as this deep thinking and pondering over what I was going to do with my life was going on as my final year of primary school (high school) was fast approaching. I was working at my part-time job at McDonald's in Chester, Virginia. (Yes - I actually worked at McDonald's.) My job usually was in the back of the restaurant, working the grill, but on this summer day, I was assigned to work the lobby for clean-up and trash duty.

I noticed a sharply dressed Soldier coming in our restaurant wearing a Maroon Beret and Jump boots. He could not have been much older than I was at 17. He explained that he was on a special duty called "hometown recruiter" for the Army. I saw him more as a peer than I would have seen as a recruiter, which definitely lowered my guard. He basically told me how much he liked being in the Army; he talked about how the Army has a lot of money to help with college, and he said that I should at least check it out. He gave me a card from the Army Recruiter with whom he worked. Well, his cool appearance and the mention of college money piqued my interest.

I called the Army Recruiter on that card and started a conversation for consideration of joining the Army. I told my dad about what I was doing. He was supportive of the idea. My father was a Marine and he served in the Korean War when he was in High School. My older brother had served in the Army for a 4-year stint. All my father's brothers served in the Navy during World War II with one of his brothers also serving the Korean War and the Vietnam War. We were not a military family per se, but we definitely love our country and believe in service. I went to the recruiting station and went over the different possibilities. I was asked to take the ASVAB and a physical so the recruiter could see what I could qualify for. I took the test and the physical and did quite well in both. When I went to the recruiter, I asked for something in electronics. I was told that I could sign up for Infantry and change my job (the army term is Military Occupational Specialty (MOS)) to something else later. I trusted this was good information, so I went to my father to sign for me. I wanted to enjoy some summer fun after I graduated high school, so I signed up 363 days in advance to start my army service in mid-July 1985. I went on my way to enjoy my senior year of high school.

During my senior year, my cousin Laura (who is really like a sister) met a young army wife (her name is Marina) at a club and told me that her husband, who was in the army, was coming home for Christmas leave. She set it up with Marina so I could go and meet Marina's husband to talk about the army. He asked me what I was signing up to do.

When I told him Infantry, he asked me what my GT score was on my ASVAB. After I told him, he asked me if I just wanted to do the "hooah stuff" and be in the Infantry. I told him what the recruiter told me about signing up for infantry and then changing later and that I wanted to be in electronics. Marina's husband told me that I was given bad information. I told my father, and he immediately called the recruiting station. My dad threatened a Congressional complaint. The lead recruiter took over my case and brought me in for a redo. He said that he would still have to keep my original date on entry or sooner, but the problem was I had to wait until I graduated high school so there was a one-month window. I finally was able to secure a job in electronics, but I had to leave after only one week after graduation – June 17, 1985.

What I did in the US Army – Part One

My MOS I was assigned was 31E – Field Radio Repairer. The title changed a few times but basically, I worked in a Communications and Electronics (C&E) shop in maintenance units. My job was to repair the radios that were used in vehicles, carried by hand, and in some special radio communication trailers. Army folks might recognize the radios in CUCVs, and later HMMWVs called RT-524, and the hand-held radios in the PRC-77 configuration. The special communication trailers were called RATT rigs. As radios were modified and improved, I worked on

SINCGARs radios. I was stationed in Ft. Knox, KY, Ft. Davis, Panama, and Ft. Campbell, KY in my first 6 years and 9 months. I was promoted in a normal time frame – not slow, but definitely not fast-tracked. When I was assigned to Ft. Campbell, KY, I had been married for 1 year with a son. I was assigned to 2nd Battalion, 5th Special Forces Group (Airborne). I was specifically placed in an Electronic Maintenance Shop (EMS) and assigned to a Special Forces "B" team. This team combined support personnel from EMS with Special Forces qualified Communication experts. Almost as soon as I was assigned to 2/5 SFG(A), I was promoted to Sergeant (E-5). I completed Airborne training (I had my "silver wings on my chest"), and I was having fun doing Soldier training. I did not focus on other things like college because I was too busy, and frankly, I just did not think about it in a serious way. In other words, I took a class here and there just for the promotion points – not starting a true path to a degree. I was also sent to the Staff Sergeant (E-6) board, so promotion would come before long. After all, I had the "Airborne advantage," which is a system where Airborne Soldiers in an airborne unit are provided a big advantage toward promotions.

After I completed Airborne School, my wife and I had our second son. Then, two months later, Saddam Hussein invaded Kuwait, and the build-up to Operation Desert Storm began. Up to that point, I had been traveling a lot on many TDYs (Temporary Duty) during normal times. I went to Operation Desert Storm, and it went pretty well as far as a combat tour could go, except I did lose a good friend who was KIA (killed-in-action). When I returned to Ft. Campbell from Operation Desert Storm, my ETS (End-term-of-service) date was approaching. I went to the in-service recruiter to find out my options and I was told that because of my Top-Secret clearance and my airborne status, my MOS would be coded where I would stay in Special Forces units. I loved the unit, but my family was suffering from all of the deployments and TDYs. The only way I could get out of this would be to get out of the Army.

What did I think Life would Be Like After the Army the First Time

When I seriously started the process to get out of the Army, I did not look at anything as far as VA benefits or anything like that. I was convinced that with my army training from an elite unit like 5th SFG(A) and my electronic training, I could get any job in either management/leadership or electronics, especially if I went to a nice-sized city. I always had an idea that I wanted to live in Atlanta, Georgia, so this seemed like the time to make that move. I reached out to some major corporations in Atlanta and connected with Delta Air Lines. Delta needed electronic repair support in their maintenance facility, so everything seemed like it fit.

What Life was Actually Like After the Army and Getting Back In

After I left the Army, I joined my family who moved to Atlanta a month earlier. I could not secure the job I was planning on getting at Delta because there was a rule back then (which still exists but has been waivered) that one could not start another job while still employed in the military. I had to burn up my terminal leave. I picked up a few odd jobs here and there. Interestingly, I still had military base access, so I went to Fort MacPherson in Atlanta (it has since been shut down) and noticed in an Army Times magazine that I made the cutoff score for Staff Sergeant (E-6). Oh well! As soon as my terminal leave ended in February 1992, I went to Delta Airlines who told me that there was a freeze in hiring because of the recession of 1992.

What do I do? All my plans were based on that job. No problem because I had serious management and leadership training from the Army so I could get a management job somewhere. I went all over Atlanta and could not find any jobs because I did not have a college degree. I actually checked with a recruiter to get back into the Army but the Army was not taking prior service personnel. Then one day my wife passed out at our Townhouse and was taken to the hospital by a friend. She went through several tests but was deemed ok and was released. We had no insurance. I had 100% coverage for me and my family when I was in the

Army but not now. I needed a job fast as I was now in debt for thousands of dollars. Finally, the only job I could find was as a QuikTrip (convenience store) Manager. I started that job with the idea I would do it for 3 months. I worked so hard in that job. The real money to be made was in overtime so I put my name on a list to be called on my days off for extra shift at any store in Atlanta. Remember, I was now in serious medical debt. I worked practically every day of the week. I could not get ahead. After my store was held up a second time, I realized I had enough after 15 months in a job I only to work for 3 months. I jumped over to sell cars. That was also a "dog eat dog" world of commissions and car sales. I was depressed at the loss of my career.

One day I came home from work and my wife asked me to investigate getting back in the Army. I depressingly said that I could not because I checked after I first left the Army. She told me that she called a recruiter and maybe I could get back in. We went to a recruiter who said no. Then we went to another recruiter who said that sometimes windows open for prior service. So, I retook the ASVAB and the day the recruiter came to take me to my physical, he said the window for prior service opened that day. This was in October 1993. I met with the Military Entrance Processing Station (MEPS) Army counselor. I was told that I could not get my old job back. Also, since I had to take a new job, I could only get back in if I agreed to take a reduction in rank.

Although had I stayed in, I would have been a Staff Sergeant.E-6, my DD-214 had my rank as Sergeant/E-5. I would now have to be a non-promotable Specialist/E-4 again.

What I did in the US Army – Take Two

When I sat with the MEPS Career Counselor, after hearing the news that I could not get my old job back and I would have to be reduced in rank to be allowed to come back in, I had to pray about my new choice. The Career Counselor offered me the MOSs for Cook, Tank Turret Mechanic, Light Wheel Vehicle Mechanic, and Generator Mechanic. I felt led to choose Generator mechanic/52D even though it was the poorest promoting of the four choices. I also believed I could do well quickly because I really understood schematics from my previous MOS as Radio Repairer. I was able to get back in within 6 days so on October 23, 1993, I was on my way to my school for my new MOS – Generator Mechanic. When I was on the bus to depart, my Career Counselor stopped the bus to give me one more piece of paperwork to sign which stated if I did not get promoted in 3 years I would be put out of the Army for good because I would exceed the Retention Control Point (RCP) because I was now a Specialist.

At that moment, I prayed to God for three things: (1) that I would be able to stay in long enough for retirement, (2) that

I would retire with at least a bachelor's degree (I knew that one reason I could not find employment previously) and (3) retire at least as a Master Sergeant/E-8. I was very motivated to get promoted in this new job. When I arrived at my first duty station of Ft. Bliss, Texas in March 1994, I met an E-4 52D who was being put out of the Army because he could not get promoted before the RCP and an E-5 who was being put out of the Army because he could not get promoted before the RCP for E-5. This did not look good, but I was going to get started in my new job and work on getting promoted. I went to college, took correspondence courses and took College Level Examination Program (CLEP) exams (which are free for active-duty military – another oft-unknown benefit) and added points like crazy. One year after arriving in Ft. Bliss, I was promoted to Sergeant/E-5 and one year after that, I was promoted to Staff Sergeant/E-6 (one of only three Generator Mechanics in the Army to get promoted that month).

Once I achieved E-6, I had to be moved from Ft. Bliss, so I was sent to Camp Kyle, Korea. Now I was working as a Senior Generator Mechanic and a Maintenance Shop Foreman. After my one-year tour in Korea, I requested a Inter Theater Transfer (ITT) to Rhine Ordnance Barracks (ROB), Kaiserslautern, Germany. I worked as a Chief Technical Inspector in a Maintenance Company there. I applied for and was accepted into the Army Warrant Officer

Program. I would soon become (after Warrant Officer Candidate School (WOC) school completion), an Engineer Equipment Repair Technician/919A. I was assigned to Ft. Riley, Kansas for three years. I then moved to Schofield Barracks, Hawaii for three years, where incidentally I completed the final two courses for my bachelor's degree. I also started and completed my master's degree. My final duty station was Ft. Hood, Texas where I was deployed to combat in Iraq for Operation Iraqi Freedom (OIF 05-07) with 4th Infantry Division (4th ID) and promoted in Iraq to my final rank of Chief Warrant Officer Three (CW3). I would go on to retire from the Army on July 1, 2008.

What did I think Life would Be Like After the Army the Second and Final Time

I really thought the second time getting out the Army the second time would be smoother. This time, I had a retirement check coming in and I had my master's degree. I thought the retirement process with the Army would be smooth as Ft. Hood is a huge base with a good relationship with the Veterans Administration (VA). After all, VA has a big hospital and operation in nearby Temple, Texas. I thought my 21-years plus experience, my rank and skills, and my degrees would set me up for smooth employment possibilities. I thought I could deal with VA on my own and not worry about a Veteran Service Organization to help me. I had received a warning in 2004 about tracking any major physical problems from an old Army friend (the Chaplain who performed my wedding ceremony to my wife) who was had just retired. I knew I had knee issues so I did go to sick call for that and did not stop until I could get an MRI as my friend suggested. I thought in my final physical exam, which the second part was with VA, I could report all of my issues I had all of those years with my various physical and mental shortcomings clearly brought on because of my generally hard service. DOUBLE NEGATIVE ALERT – I was never not in a go-to-war type of unit, and many of my units had harder 18th Airborne Corps or Special Operations standards of physical preparation.

What Life was Actually Like After the Army

Initially, my job situation was not bad. I was able to secure a Contract job with McLane Advanced Technologies (MAT) while I was on terminal leave. The company asked me to go to Iraq where I would eventually become the Program Manager at Joint Base Balad, Iraq. It was kind of a pain, but I felt like I was solidifying my position by making this sacrifice of living in a hard situation (still a combat zone) and being separated from my family. Admittedly, I did get a nice paycheck but what would happen would make that paycheck not worth it. I lived in Iraq for 1 year and 9 months. When I returned, it seemed like I made the right decision because the company owner recognized me for overseeing the completion of more services and repairs than ever before. A few months later, with the company magazine featuring me still laying around on cubicles, I was laid off. In fact, I was laid off on a Wednesday in the middle of the morning and marched to my car and escorted off the property like a criminal. I was now unemployed literally at a moment's notice and had to figure out what I was going to do. I did not learn the "rub elbows" method used at that company. Those people were the ones retained. Hard work, by itself, was not enough.

As far as my VA claim was going, I thought my interview would be enough. By the time my initial claim was completed, I was in Iraq. I did not know anything about this process, so I was quite surprised when my initial claim came back completely missing my issues with my knees. I appealed and was granted the knee VA disability, but I would continue to work on my VA claim even up to today. It is harder and harder to connect to my service time for their purposes. I know it's from my service time but proving it is harder as I have been separated longer. My current VA disability status in 90% (which is "VA Math") but if you added up all the percentages, I would have 230%.

How I Overcame the Misconceptions

Mistakes I Corrected for Second Transition – I learned some things about a proper transition from my first attempt at transitioning.

Degrees or other Certifications - This time I made sure I had plenty of education to support my job search outside of my military experience. If college education is not your thing, then get your Commercial Driver's License (CDL), or Electrician certification or whatever. Try to secure these extra degrees or certifications while you are in so you can use tuition assistance and save your education benefits like Post 9/11 GI Bill for later.

Employment before you depart the service – I was not allowed to accept employment while on terminal leave the first time I left the Army. I wanted to emphasize to use that Terminal Leave time to secure employment before service is over.

Overall Misconceptions and How I Overcame Them – Even with the experience of getting out and returning to the service, I still had issues and misconceptions that I learned later to overcome. My scenario was different when I exited the military the first time because this time, I was retiring so I could keep benefits of having a Military ID Card, TRICARE health care and other benefits accordingly. There were still several misconceptions I had to overcome to include VA service claims, finding the right Veteran Service Organization, choosing the Survivor Benefit Plan (SBP) versus life insurance, and where to live for use of benefits.

VA service claims – This starts before you leave the military because that action of reporting medical issues "service connected." With your last two years of the military, do a thorough inspection of your health and do not dismiss anything. Do you have allergies? Do you have asthma issues? Is your back hurting? Do you sleep well? Do not dismiss anything. This can affect the rest of your life. An overall VA disability rating of 50% or higher can really set you up well if you can qualify for that.

Finding the right Veteran Service Organization (VSO) – VSOs are organizations that have a direct connection with VA who can advise and assist for advice and help make claims to VA. There are many VSOs at a national level to include Disabled American Veterans (DAV), Veterans of Foreign Wars (VFW), and American Legion to name a few of more than 10 national organizations. If you live in Texas, there is the Texas Veterans Commission (TVC), which is the VSO I use. Even after you find a good VSO, you also want to have a good Veteran Service Representative (VSR) person who is supportive and really wants to help you get all the benefits you have coming to you. Ask around where you live and find good VSOs and meet with them 1 year before you depart from the military to get the relationship started. I heard DAV is very good and some tell me VFW is good so you should ask around. I currently have Mr. Hans Madsen from TVC representing me as my VSR and he is excellent in his service and advice. I must say, if you live in Texas, TVC has an office located in the State Capitol. TVC is very well connected in Texas and fights for expansion of rights for veterans in Texas.

Choosing the Survivor Benefit Plan (SBP) versus life insurance – This is a decision that everyone who is retiring should make. SBP must be done at the time of retirement. Look up the benefits and problems with SBP and decide. SBP is a good plan but can be pricy and does not cover single people with no children. Basically, SBP will give your spouse at the time of your death annuity payments, but SBP beneficiaries cannot be changed so if the beneficiary dies before you, the money goes nowhere. This is a discussion for each individual couple and family to have. I decided to secure a very good whole life insurance policy.

Where to live for use of benefits – Sometimes you go where you secure employment, so that is one thing. However, if you can plan, try to keep in mind that if you are close to a base somewhere, you can access the Commissary, PX/BX, Gyms, Medical, and many other services. It is nice. On a bigger scale, the State you live in can have additional benefits for military. I think Texas has as much, or more, benefits as any State. For example, in Texas, if you are a Disabled Veteran (DV) with DV license plate, you can park at the airport for free. So, consider where you will live as part of your planning for transition.

Final thoughts – By reading my story and this book, you are already ahead of the learning curve as to how you can be successful in your transition. Find veterans, like you see in this book, and talk to them before you depart the service, if you can, or any time after. We learn so much from each other. If you are reading this and you served, thank you for your service. If you are reading this for a loved one who served, thank you for your support. I mentioned that my home is now in Texas. In reality, with all of my moves, as I am from VA and now live in TX, my 'home' is wherever my wife is.

This We'll Defend!!

DAVID AMMONS, PHD

ARMY

CW3 (USA, RET)

Dr.daveammons16@gmail.com

Ph: 413-828-3725

NOTE on Title: My rank when I retired from the Army was as a Chief Warrant Officer Three (CW3). I was not a Helicopter Pilot. I was a technician specializing in maintenance for engineering equipment and managing motor pools. In the Army, Warrant Officers (who are technicians, not pilots) are called "Chief" as a nickname. This is like how many in the Army refer to a unit First Sergeant as "Top." Army Pilot Warrant Officers, as well as Navy and Marine Warrant Officers, are not called "Chief." I was often called Chief A or Chief Ammons.

RESOURCES

American Legion

The American Legion was chartered by Congress in 1919 as a patriotic veteran's organization. Focusing on service to veterans, service members, and communities, the Legion evolved from a group of war-weary veterans of World War I into one of the most influential nonprofit groups in the United States. Membership swiftly grew to over 1 million, and local posts sprang up across the country. Today, membership is over 1.6 million in more than 12,000 posts worldwide. The posts are organized into 55 departments: one for each of the 50 states, along with the Districts of Columbia, Puerto Rico, France, Latin America, and the Philippines.

Over the years, the Legion has built its identity by achieving hundreds of benefits and services for veterans, supporting the U.S. Armed Forces, and instilling the values of responsible citizenship among young people. From the nation-changing of The American Legion-drafted GI Bill to relief for veterans exposed to toxic contamination in the service, veterans of The American Legion have worked for over a century to improve and strengthen the nation they swore with their lives to defend.

https://www.legion.org/

Army Transition Assistance Program

The Army Transition Assistance Program (TAP) is the Army's Transition Program responsible for providing soldiers with the counseling, employment, and education workshops, and seminars required to achieve the law and policy Career Readiness Standards (CRS) mandated compliance. TAP has undergone re-engineering to "prepare" and "connect" soldiers to ensure the greatest opportunities for successful personal and career achievement upon transition from active duty.

https://myarmybenefits.us.army.mil/Benefit-Library/Federal-Benefits/Army-Transition-Assistance-Program-(TAP)-

Azimuth

Their mission is to connect veterans to services. It's pretty straightforward. There are thousands of programs and services available to vets and their families, as well as thousands of vets who need and want help. They build a bridge to connect them. They keep this mission first and foremost in all our efforts.

Founder Matt Hall
thefirstmatthall@gmail.com
https://azimuth.org/

Choose to L;ve

Some rare individuals transform personal adversity into a powerful force for change; Alicia Nolan is such a person. Leading Choose to L;VE, LLC, she advocates for mental health and suicide prevention, inspired by her journey. With a strong educational foundation and certifications in Master Resiliency Training, Mental Health First Aid, and Question Persuade Refer Gatekeeper, Alicia champions change, supported by the "It Starts With Me" Award.

Choose to L;VE, LLC, symbolized by the semicolon, raises awareness through products supporting the Pikes Peak Suicide Prevention Partnership. This initiative reflects Alicia's commitment to societal impact stemming from the loss of her wife. Her mission is to advocate for mental health reform and inspire resilience.

https://choosetolive.org/

DoD TAP Transition Assistance Program

DoD TAP is an outcome-based statutory program (10 USC, Ch. 58) that bolsters opportunities, services, and training for transitioning Service members in their preparation to meet post-military goals.

The mandatory components of TAP are applicable to all Service members who have at least 180 continuous days or more on active duty, including the National Guard and Reserve.

The DoD Military-Civilian Transition Office (MCTO) was formed in January 2020 due to a merger between the Office for Reintegration Programs and the Transition to Veterans Program Office under the Defense Human Resources Activity to provide streamlined services to members of the Armed Forces and their families.

MCTO is responsible for designing, overseeing, and evaluating TAP and provides transition assistance policy and program oversight to promote, advance, and instill a culture of career-ready Service members.

MCTO's mission is to continually improve the delivery of resources, information, and assistance provided through the programs, promoting their effective and efficient support of transitioning Service members and members of the National Guard and Reserve, their families, and communities worldwide.

https://www.dodtap.mil/dodtap/app/home

Mental Health – Veterans Administration (VA)

Visit this site to view stories from Veterans of all service eras who have successfully dealt with transitioning from service and overcoming mental health challenges. MakeTheConnection.net is a one-stop resource where Veterans and their families and friends can privately explore information on mental health issues, hear fellow Veterans and their families share their stories of resilience, and easily find and access the support and resources they need.

https://www.mentalhealth.va.gov/transitioning-service/resources.asp

Military Child Well-Being Toolkit

The MCEC Military Child Well-Being Toolkit provides social-emotional support resources for parents, educators, school counselors, administrators, and professionals who work with military-connected youth. It draws from recognized resources and approaches, including:

The Collaborative for Academic, Social, and Emotional Learning (CASEL)

- Whole Child Design
- Social Emotional Academic Development (S.E.A.D.)
- The U.S. Surgeon General's 2021 Advisory on Youth Mental Health

The Toolkit's evidence-based content fosters emotional intelligence (EI), mindfulness, and overall well-being for military children. It offers resources for families living with post-traumatic stress disorder (PTSD), traumatic brain injury (TBI), and other injuries. There are also resources on suicide prevention and awareness, LGBTQIA+, and diversity/equity/inclusion/social justice.

https://militarychild.org/resource/wellbeing-toolkit/

Military One Source

Military OneSource can help you set goals, learn about the benefits you've earned, explore education opportunities, get ready for the civilian workforce, and offer a range of additional resources to meet your needs. Get personalized support from Military OneSource to help you navigate your transition from military life to civilian life today.

https://www.militaryonesource.mil/transition-retirement/separation/transition-assistance-programs-and-resources/

Military Transition

Their work helps service members, veterans, spouses, and employers better understand and prepare for the military-to-civilian transition process and civilian employment. They are a group of independent veterans who have already transitioned. Our service ranges from less than five to more than twenty years in uniform as officers and enlisted members.

https://www.military-transition.org/resources.html

PTSD – Veterans Administration (VA)

When someone has PTSD, it affects family and friends too. As loved ones, you spend time and energy to support your partner, family member, or friend with PTSD. Learn about resources for your self-care while helping a loved one with PTSD.

Learning about PTSD helps you to understand what your loved one is experiencing. But you need to take care of yourself too. Your support network — family, friends, and health providers — is a good place to start, but don't be afraid to reach out beyond that close circle. Here are some resources that can help.

https://www.ptsd.va.gov/family/support_family_friends.asp

The Warrior 110

The Warrior 110 program raises awareness and funds for veterans suffering from physical and emotional ailments such as PTS (post-traumatic stress) and TBI (traumatic brain injury).

Awareness and dollars are raised through "Ruck Marches" (weighted walks often used in military training that stretch for more miles) and various other events throughout the year.

Their mission is to help support America's Vets who live with psychological, emotional, and physical issues stemming from service to OUR country!

https://thewarrior110.org/

Veterans Administration (VA)

VA's Veterans Health Administration is the largest integrated health care network in the United States, with 1,255 health care facilities serving 9 million enrolled Veterans each year.

https://www.va.gov/

VA Rep Indy - Stephanie D. Sanchez = Stephanie.Sanchez@va.gov

Wounded Warrior Project

Wounded Warrior Project (WWP) began in 2003 as a small, grassroots effort providing simple care and comfort items to the hospital bedsides of the first wounded service members returning home from the conflicts in Iraq and Afghanistan. As their post-service needs evolved, so have our programs and services. Today, through our direct programs in mental health, career counseling, and long-term rehabilitative care, along with our advocacy efforts, we improve the lives of millions of warriors and their families.

https://www.woundedwarriorproject.org